Also by Baron Perlman

*Come Collect with Me: Musings on Collecting
and American Antiques*

*The Collector's World: More Musings on Collecting
and American Antiques*

REFLECTIONS ON COLLECTING

Still Musing on Collecting and American Antiques

Baron Perlman

CKBooks Publishing

Publisher's Cataloging-in-Publication Data

Names: Perlman, Baron, 1946- , author.

Title: Reflections on collecting : still musing on collecting and American antiques / Baron Perlman.

Description: New Glarus, WI : CKBooks Publishing, 2025. | Series: Musings on collecting series ; 3. | Includes index. | Includes 35 color photos. | Summary: Barry Perlman, a long-time contributing columnist to the Maine Antique Digest, explains what makes collectors tick, explores the decisions and emotions of the collector's experience, and the discoveries, wanderings, and wonder of collecting, including the pitfalls, luck, joy, failures, desire...and quitting collecting.

Identifiers: LCCN 2025903880 | ISBN 9781966219071 (hardcover) | ISBN9781966219088 (pbk.) | ISBN 9781966219064 (ebook)

Subjects: LCSH: Collectors and collecting – United States. | Antiques – United States. | Antiques – Psychological aspects. | Decorative arts – Collectors and collecting – United States. | BISAC: ANTIQUES & COLLECTIBLES / General. | ANTIQUES & COLLECTIBLES / Buying & Selling / General. | ANTIQUES & COLLECTIBLES / Subjects & Themes / General.

Classification: LCC NK1125.P47 2025 | DDC 745.10973--dc23

LC record available at https://lccn.loc.gov/2025903880

Cover Painting: Thomas Chambers,
                    A View of the Hudson from West Point
Photographer: Ken Cravillion · kgcphoto.com

CKBooks Publishing
P.O. Box 214
New Glarus, WI
53574
ckbookspublishing.com

To John—Collector, Dealer, Auctioneer, and Friend—
for your support, and interest in collectors
and their wonderful journeys

TABLE OF CONTENTS

FOREWORD

When Baron Perlman invited me to write the foreword for this book, I was honored, of course. I also expected it to be a simple task—after all, words are my business. Having spent the better part of my adult life running an art, antiques, and collectibles auction house where 15k - 20k items are sold each year, I have written, edited, and spoken *a lot* of words. For a few years, I ventured away from my auction career and served as the Editor in Chief of a regional luxury magazine (another job involving lots of words), where I wrote about topics like travel, food, design, philanthropy, and naturally, antiques and collecting. So, writing a book forward would be a piece of cake, I told myself (and Barry). Wrong. Writer's block is real. I am pretty sure Dante's tenth circle was a blank page, a pen, and a mandate to compose something semi-coherent every day for the rest of eternity. In terms of drafting this forward, the mental block had less to do with knowing where to start and more to do with knowing where to *end*.

The essays and publications Barry has undertaken to produce epitomize collecting as the team sport it is, as illustrated by the title of his first book: *Come Collect with Me* (emphasis on the with). Without other collectors, there would be no benchmarking of what is hot and what is not, no thrill of finding a rarity that no one else has yet uncovered, no one else to understand the lengths to which we have gone to fill a vacant spot in our collection. An entire industry was created, and has evolved, to serve the changing needs of collectors in every category. Barry's nuanced insights into the unique world of collecting are an incredible opportunity to understand, and possibly identify with a community who has stumbled upon a mystical, magical intersection of history, aesthetic, competition, investigation, curiosity, passion, and wonder.

For me, there is no other industry quite like the one that caters to the collecting world. To sum it up in a few paragraphs is impossible. My job allows me to interact with collectors throughout the phases of their pursuits—from the first-time buyer to the aficionado, from the avocationalist to the career-professional. My team and I deliver purchases and pack up entire collections, and I have visited hundreds, if not thousands of collectors' homes. Every visit is a new adventure —an opportunity to see or learn something new. My late business partner used to say, "It's like Christmas every day."

Someone once asked me which I like more, the people I serve or the objects I sell. It is an impossible question to answer. Without one, there is not the other—and each of them (person and object) has a story to tell. In listening to their stories, I have gained a bevy of friends, a wealth of knowledge, a growing curiosity, an abundance of joy, and a lifetime of memories.

I encourage you to read each of the books in this series— and learn how and why collecting can change your life. Come collect *with* Barry and me. You won't regret it.

Amelia Jeffers
Columbus, Ohio

ACKNOWLEDGMENTS

At a point last year, I realized I had enough content for a third volume on collecting and American antiques. But the ideas for this book did not arise with me alone. I had help, lots of it, and it is to those individuals that I owe a deep debt of gratitude.

I think of dealers, fellow collectors, and others to whom I reached out and who reached out to me: Amelia, Arthur, Clayton, David H., David L. again, and David S. yet again, Don, Helaine, Jan, Jeffrey, Jim. John, Kevin, Michael, Nathaniel, Peter, Robert, and Suzanne to name just a few. Their observations and experiences with collectors and American antiques com-plemented and surpassed my own and added validity and life to what I was trying to appreciate and understand.

I was fortunate some years ago to be given the opportunity to pen a column for the national publication, *Maine Antique Digest* (MAD). Doing so kept me in touch with collectors and dealers in the American antique universe. One outcome was having ideas and topics tossed my way on a regular basis. "When are you going to broach the issue of?" Or "Can I look forward to a column about ... ?" Chapters 1, 3, 7, 12, 13, 15, 16, 17, 20, 21, 25, 26, 27, 28, 29, 30 were published in *MAD* and appear in modified form.

Clayton Pennington, Editor of *Maine Antique Digest* and his staff are wonderful in their support, fact finding, and enjoyment of holiday chocolates.

I have thanked him in the past, and my dear friend Tom Herzing continues to be a font of ideas and a muse for my writing. His creativity and way with words consistently teaches me what it means to write well.

Applause for Ken Cravillion. The photographs are his. He has a keen eye and a wonderful sense of perspective and design.

Collectors also have responded to my website: Comecollectwithme.com, with their ideas and support as do collectors waiting in line for shows to open with whom I avidly talk, and those who email me.

I must thank my readers, both of my first two books *Come Collect with Me* and *The Collector's World*, my columns in *Maine Antique Digest* and my website and blog. Thanks for sticking with me. I hope that what you have read here resonates with you.

My wife Sandy is a wonderful sounding board for ideas and turns of the phrase, and my eldest son Nathaniel has always been supportive and interested in the writing and antiques I use as exemplars. Despite the notion that younger folks are not interested in antiques, he has dibs on several in our collection.

Our two cats, Roscoe and Quimby, are examples that antiques are meant to be lived with, and I cannot think of a single table, desk or other surface, and chairs galore they have not made their own.

To all who have contributed and whom I have failed to mention, I apologize. This book would not exist without you.

PREFACE

I have collected my entire life—stamps, coins, comic books, and baseball cards as a preteen and then teen. When I met my (to be) wife Sandy more than 50 years ago, American antiques took center stage with her in the lead. Five decades of devotion to one focused love is bound to lead to lessons learned, and I found I had learned quite a bit. My vocation—practicing clinical psychology on myself and others—led to discoveries, revelations and even surprises. In brief, I have experienced a lifetime of collector wonderings and wanderings. I drew conclusions. There were even moments I thought I had figured it out, the way Wall Street guys do in novels, only to find everything is a maybe instead of a certainty.

Though I have retired from my profession as a university professor, I have kept in contact with my colleagues. They have offered insights, fresh perspectives, refinements, contradictions, and even confirmation of some of my own insights. Much of what I taught in the classroom or applied in therapy became grist for my collecting mill.

I have always thought of myself as speaking for collectors—not dealers, auction houses, or museums. All are important mind you, but I have striven to bring collectors center stage—why they do what they do, what they are thinking, even how they cope with inevitable disappointments—and put them in the spotlight.

The inception for this book began in illness. Its roots were planted 55 years ago in Vietnam. Repeated exposure to Agent Orange is not a good thing. As treatment began and progressed, I found myself taking stock of what was truly important to me. Activities that once had demanded my attention fell by the wayside. Over time, it became apparent what pursuits and daily events I could not surrender.

Family and friends were high on my list. Staying connected is crucial to my wellbeing. The morning ritual of reading the newspaper with a mug of tea is imperative. Being physically able to do spring household and yard work was a delight. Who was happier than me washing windows? Winnowing and sifting what gave my life meaning was that collecting was not only important to me but somehow both humanizing and fulfilling.

At the same time, I have loved books my entire life. I love the way they feel, smell, and the sound they make when a page is turned. So why not make a book revealing my musings and thoughts about collecting (and American antiques)?

I have done so twice now. Each time, I sat back from the keyboard with a sigh. I believed that I had covered the waterfront of collecting.

Yes, I was mistaken, and this book is the result of that unfounded certainty. It is both personal and objective. The pieces described and pictured are from our personal collection, and yes, there are magnificent antiques out there I would love to own. Somebody else with more money at a more propitious time beat me to them. My own mistakes let a few escape as well.

The items pictured are ones that moved me, that inspired thoughts and even opened my appreciation. Detailed information about each may be found in *Descriptions of Pictured Pieces* at the end of the book. Certainly, better examples exist for many of the genres shown, but these are the antiques with which we live. Each image is meant to elaborate on and bring to life a chapter's content. The description of the antique and story that accompanies it may at times interrupt the flow of the chapter's text and, therefore, I have set off this text to advise the reader of such.

If I refer to Sandy, that is my wife and fellow collector. Some antiques I discuss in this book also appeared in *Come Collect with Me* but there they served different purposes. If there are any errors in describing the antiques pictured you can lay the responsibility at my doorstep—although I would like to believe the dealers who provided information, or the auction houses, etc. might bear a bit of culpability but the buck (information) stops with me.

In 2019 *Come Collect with Me: Musings on Collecting and American Antiques* was completed. Style and connoisseurship criteria were central to my musings. I interwove these criteria with antiques Sandy and I have in our collection. I applied them more broadly to the world of collectors of American antiques. Much of what I have to say here (and there, I believe) applies to collectors of Barbie dolls, bobbleheads, sewing machines, or classic cars. Collectors are individuals driven by sundry aspirations, more or less able to pursue and possess. I write about what they have in common: hopes, dreams, experiences, failures, disappointments.

The Collectors World: More Musings on Collecting and American Antiques appeared in 2021. Again, I thought I was done, Finis, with discussions of collecting. I was wrong for a second time. I should have known better and made peace with the errors in my thinking. In *The Collector's World* I wrote of emotions, self-reflection, lessons to be learned, and shared a wish or two in ending.

So now I offer Volume Three to remedy past omissions. This time I do not delude myself: Mine is a journey that is never done. I am happy with that. These are, modestly, my *Reflections on Collecting*. The insights keep coming, and I find fulfillment and pleasure in sharing them. I am sure I have, as Frost said, "Miles to go before I sleep." And "... promises to keep," to myself if no one else. There are more famous trilogies in the literature world: Shakespeare's *Henry IV, Part*

I, Henry IV, Part II and *Henry V* or *Lord of the Rings* are just two. Of them I add this unassuming tome to the list.

Baron Perlman
Oshkosh, WI, 2025

P.S. I hope you enjoy this book. If so, reviews are greatly appreciated. Connect with me at my website: Comecollectwithme.com. You can also follow me on Facebook and Instagram.

INTRODUCTION

I am not alone. For many collectors, the act of collecting is central to their lives and well-being. It is a journey I (and they) would not miss. I find myself in the world of American antiques. It is a universe that is simultaneously complex, fascinating, frustrating, and euphoric. It is a world that encapsulates and captures what it means "to live."

What will the reader find in Reflections on Collecting? I felt compelled to look at collectors' experiences with the highs and lows. I know that my own personality affects my collecting and the topic merits discussion. I had to talk about beauty (aesthetic appreciation). I like most (all?) collectors find the genres I am drawn to beautiful. They pluck at my heart strings. A good double play in baseball is beautiful, as is a gorgeous fleeting spring morning in Wisconsin. And so is a Connecticut highchair from the middle of the 18th century.

This appreciation for aesthetics coupled with a delight for history makes me a natural to collect what you will find pictured and sought after. I woke up one morning years ago to the realization that collecting encompassed both my heart and soul—a benevolent condition I could not live without. Throughout my contemplations put down on paper, I tried for a tone that is readable, light, fun. Do not assume that "reflections" are dry stuff to be numbered and elucidated. They are anything but.

Yet collectors vary in what they find beautiful. What pulls at my heart may be blah to someone else. It is their hearts and souls that define each collector's and their collections' identity, some mainstream, others eccentric.

Objects have the power to move us, to define a generation. A fine example would be the 1945 photo of the sailor kissing and embracing a nurse in Times Square in a celebration of the end of World War II on V-J Day. As would a photo of Woodstock (Music and Art Fair) in 1969. Or a Model T Ford, the wonderment of St. Paul's Cathedral or Westminster Abbey, or a Colt revolver that defined the West. American antiques have that power over me. They give me meaning and understanding of America before and after it became a nation, and the lives its citizens led.

Did I know the importance collecting would hold for me when I first started? I most certainly did not. Would any neophyte collector persevere if in the face of failure, suffering, regrets, and an empty bank account? Counterbalancing these are love, desire, awe, joy, gratitude, and devotion. I have learned to be kind to myself, to forgive my foibles that sometimes are my undoing as a collector. All collectors make mistakes, and I take solace in this truth as I have made my fair share of them.

Collectors do not go about their business in a vacuum. My successes and failures were and are influenced by a wide variety of variables. Serendipity is but one such example. And I have been wooed, feeling as if someone had cast a spell upon me. Sex as part of collecting? Look at the chapter on seduction and draw your own conclusions.

The hard work of developing connoisseurship, however, is just a beginning. Collectors need to listen to their hearts and follow where those feelings lead. The pictured Hudson Valley paintings (Chapters 7, 11, 14) are but one of thousands of scenes depicted in America. Yet I was enraptured and captured by them.

I attempt to bring substance and vitality to something that is one of the most significant parts of my and many people's lives. Let us puzzle together with the broader and deeper meaning of the subject, in our case collecting. And more specifically as an exemplar, the collecting of American antiques.

I hope my passion is evident. I try to illuminate the adventure, a wonderful adventure, that I have been on. For collecting truly is an adventure as rousing as a John Phillips Sousa march, an adventure for the ages.

'Nuff said. Enjoy.

CHAPTER 1

Aesthetic Appreciation

I offered my opinion in *The Collector's World* (2021) that the two primary reasons people collect is the endeavor brings them happiness or fulfilment, perhaps both. Over time I have adopted either a corrected or more nuanced view. Some collectors are driven by what may simply be termed "aesthetic appreciation," a romance with the objects themselves. Admittedly, we usually dismiss statements such as, "I love that chair" as social frothing, politeness or exaggeration, but the fact remains: The visual historical and tactile characteristics of fine antiques capture something in our character that is powerfully compelling.

I see it in myself. The composition and how the colors pop in a wonderful Hudson Valley painting. The perfect form, fans, and surface of a dropfront desk. An exquisite silver teapot that I could stare at for hours (pictured in Chapter 20). A candlestand that is beautiful. In all these cases, the craftsman has created a work that surpasses most others of the genre, something beautiful in every way.

The candlestand has wonderful proportions and therefore does not "squat" as it sits on the floor. It is a gorgeous New England, probably New Hampshire or Maine piece. The surface bears its original paint. And the *piece de resistance* is the fact that the design on its top is not inlay but paint.

The candlestand is an extremely successful vernacular expression of the early neoclassical style in America. A similar paint decorated tilt-top candlestand is in the collection of the Henry Ford Museum in Dearborn, Michigan. It is also illustrated in Dean Fales, Jr., American Painted Furniture 1660-1680. Our candlestand is arguably a more successful design. The elements of its characteristics create a stand that exceeds the sum of its parts. It is a gorgeous American antique.

The fact that a museum has a similar stand, and that ours may be better, causes me as a collector to puff my chest out a bit. A museum has given its seal of approval, has verified our fine taste, I tell myself. That may be right on or irrational, of course, since museum holdings vary from exquisite to average. None the less, it adds to and may deepen the story about the candlestand, depending on what documentation and research the museum has in hand. At the least, it may help someone in the future determine the stands' craftsman. (Detailed information about the candlestand and all antiques pictured may be found at the book's end in *Descriptions of Pictured Pieces*.)

The word "aesthetics" comes from the Greek *aisthanomai*, which means to perceive. It involves the valuing of something beautiful—typically art, music, antiques, literature, or dance—but the feeling could even be inspired by the beauty of a perfectly turned double play in baseball, Michael Jordan soaring through the air in basketball, a classic car so Art Deco that one forgets it is a machine, or a pair of high heel shoes. Aesthetics implies and endorses a concern for beauty. The painting I refer to by Thomas Chambers (see its image in the chapter Awe), creates a mood or overall feeling most of its genre do not. The artist has created a harmony of color and shapes, or the opposite, a tension in his painting that the viewer can feel. The consequence is that my breath is taken away, I am fascinated, in awe, experience a sense of transcendence, wonder, and admiration.

That means (and you may have already reached this conclusion) that some people are not struck by the good looks and elegance in the same piece of artwork or antique I find so compelling. The cliché does not lie, beauty is in the eye of the beholder. You and I get to decide what we find beautiful. While some works create a sense of aesthetic perfection in almost every viewer or listener (The Mona Lisa for example, or Beethoven's 9th Symphony), we know that the appreciation of American antiques and many other genres is learned, not inherent or inevitable. Classic music that makes hearts beat faster and the listener believe in the genius of man and angels above may have originally been panned as strident, too *avant-garde*, or at odds with prevailing cultural definitions of beauty, and thus in its own day denied admiration. (Beethoven's 9th is an exception, receiving five standing ovations at its inaugural performance at Vienna's Theater am Kärntnertor that the composer did not hear because he composed the piece and conducted the orchestra while stone deaf.)

How does our aesthetic appreciation develop? To say that we are brainwashed is too blunt, incomplete, and simplistic, yet it contains within it a kernel of truth. Teachers, whoever we allow to be our mentors, instruct us to actively observe, feel, and experience the world around us—art, nature, sports, and yes, antiques. One well-known dealer said those of his ilk were teachers who "cultivate that delight and wonderment, not instill it. I think it starts with a general sense of curiosity, but it works best if there is some interest inside a person. I suppose occasionally there is a conversion of a true non-believer; however, that must be rare." How the curiosity is born remains somewhat a mystery, and probably differs aficionado to aficionado.

My wife took ballet lessons for decades and told me that a ballerina should look like she is lifting off the floor as she lands. She has applied that criterion to 18th century candlestands ever since we began collecting. Ones that "squat," to use her term, she finds unattractive while those that soar, she likes. The candlestand pictured in this chapter represents her views in this matter of taste. If she were your teacher when you learned about such pieces, she would have informed and enlightened you in what it is you should look for. Thus, she would have planted within you a sense of beauty for the form, and a language to describe it. And she had taught me to appreciate, to value, and in a way, to understand what something I might have thought inanimate can be sprightly, light, and intensely artistic.

For we are indeed taught a vocabulary of aesthetics. We learn "artspeak," "antiquespeak," "musicspeak," or "carspeak." Think of antique American furniture. One speaks of the form, dimensions, patina, and craftsmanship, to name merely a few of its attributes. If the following antiquespeak sets your heart aflutter and you can picture the chair in question, you are a true Americana lover. Note the way the language is used to humanize the object. We are accustomed to think of objects as having "legs," but "knees" and "feet" make the thing more a part of our world. I quote from Peter Eaton's *Maine Antique Digest* advertisement in the December 15, 2021, issue (with his permission).

An exceptional Chippendale chair having a scrolled crest rail with rolled ends and centered by a carved scallop shell, and a pierced and interwoven splat. The through-tenoned shaped seat rail has a molded edge, the knee returns have carved volutes at the ends, and the knees are shell-carved. The beautifully proportioned cabriole legs end in boldly-carved ball and claw feet. The rear legs are fully chamfered below the seat rail. The original seat frame is yellow pine. Cherry throughout in a rich old surface. There is an old crack at the juncture of the seat rail and the right rear (facing) leg. In the same collection for the last forty years. Probably Philadelphia area, but possibly central Connecticut because of the use of cherry as a primary wood. Seat 18," 41 ½" height.

For a listing of the style and connoisseurship criteria by which to judge American antiques see *Come Collect with Me*, page 13. On occasion they are mixed together just right, and a beautiful piece is created.

On a completely different level, if you are a classic car collector this description may well raise your heart rate.

Nineteen sixty-nine GTO, red with black interior. The '69 marks the cleanest expression of this A-body generation (hidden head-lights and Endura nose, no front vent windows). Thirty-two thousand original miles. Two owner vehicle, number matching, frame-off rotisserie restoration. Award winning. Ram Air IV rated at 370 hp at 5,500 rpm and 445 lb-ft at 3,900 rpm of torque featuring special header-like high-flow exhaust manifolds, high-flow cylinder heads, a specific high-rise aluminum intake manifold, hydraulic lifters, larger Rochester Quadrajet four-barrel carburetor, high-lift/long-duration cam-shaft. Muncie four-speed transmission. Bucket seats, center console, AM-FM stereo radio with 8-trach tape player, power antenna, rally gauge cluster, custom steering wheel, red-line tires and hood tachometer.

Aesthetic appreciation can have an intellectual as well as an emotional component. There exist less-than-stellar pieces of furniture made by famous Philadelphia craftsmen. To some collectors it is the maker, not necessarily the form, that drives their lust and esteem for the object. Many would say, "nonsense." At the same time matched sets of Philadelphia formal chairs for placement around a dining room table fetch more than a pretty penny and are loved and coveted by a certain cadre of collectors. I, however, do not find them beautiful even when I can elucidate their merits, for they do not tug at my heart. Even with the right teacher I do not believe I would change my mind. (Truth in disclosure: I would rather own the car than such chairs.)

The aesthetic appreciation difference between lovers of these chairs and me is not due to my preferences having been frozen in time. I have started collecting new genres—at least for me—in the last decade and find them beautiful to behold. The song, "Love Makes the World Go Round" from the musical *Carnival* for our purposes might as well have been titled *Aesthetic Appreciation Makes the World Go Round*. That is why subsets of collectors swoon over and love so many different classes of objects and discover new genres to swoon over as well.

Generalizing from my wife's ballet metaphor and feelings about candlestands, those from whom we learn aesthetic appreciation do more than teach us to notice the world and our feelings or lend us a vocabulary to describe the beautiful. They also model for us the aesthetic in their responses to certain objects. A dealer may have many pieces in her shop and show booth, most of which she will gladly extol. But if you ask her what is truly special, she knows immediately the few antiques she wants to show you. Her demeanor may change, be more subdued in the presence of something that awes, or she may become effusively excited. "Look at this," she will say as she shows you the sheer perfection in the simplicity of a Shaker box or the harmony of the stones, setting and gestalt in a piece of Edwardian jewelry.

Eventually, as all collectors do, we become enchanted by special pieces in the genres we collect, and almost without knowing it, find that our aesthetic appreciation becomes unconscious and instinctive. We know a beautiful object when we see it, only putting in words afterwards why it is so. This is what the book *Blink* is about. In looking back, I can pinpoint the moment when this became true of my wife and me. Bernice Miller, a dealer who mentored us, had in her inventory a New England tallcase clock we had only seen in photographs. We walked right by it when we were in her home. "This could not be the same clock we had seen photographs of," we said to ourselves, for it was too beautiful. If you had told me only a few years prior that I would find a tallcase clock beautiful I would have laughed at the suggestion. I laugh no more and have not since that aesthetic experience decades ago. (A photograph of this tallcase clock can be found in *Come Collect with Me*). We now own three.

If we interpret and learn to define beauty in the world, does it exist "out there" independent of our perceptions? The answer may be "yes" although I am not on firm philosophical ground when I say this. I am told that all cultures find flowers beautiful, for example. Looking at them gives almost everyone pleasure—their shape, colors fragrance, and sense of fragility. Theories exist for their perceived beauty. The same may hold in the world of architecture and buildings. Some buildings utilizing the "golden ratio" appear more balanced, and we find them more beautiful than others with different elements. Architects of all types take advantage of the golden ratio. Rather than a lengthy explanation I will let you find one, if you are so motivated, that makes sense to you. In brief, we may be hardwired to find certain objects more beautiful than others.

Some philosophers consider beauty the ultimate value. We pursue beauty for its own sake, needing to be in its presence. Beauty is good. While I do not drink coffee, I have heard those who do describe a perfect cup of java as beautiful—the aroma, the taste, the pleasure. There are times when I feel the same way about a cup of tea. Time stops and I am transported somewhere else. My entire existence becomes the cup of Darjeeling I nestle in my hands.

What I am describing is the feeling of being fully absorbed when in the presence of beauty, like others' descriptions of flow. A good book with a wonderful use of language takes us elsewhere. I have been at crowded, noisy antique shows and stopped dead in my tracks by a beautiful object. People disappear, what they are saying disappears. I am alone in the presence of something with a feeling akin to the hushed reverence of being in a house of worship. Collectors live for the moments they are fully absorbed in the presence of beauty.

Of course, complex reasons exist for beautiful objects being defined as such. But as I noted, our initial reaction to something beautiful is one of simplicity. The object simply is beautiful. We can deconstruct our *Blink* moment later, putting into words, "antiquespeak," as to why the piece of furniture or painting belongs in a museum or commands the price it does. But prior to the deconstruction we simply know it knocks us for a loop.

I touched lightly on an important point when I said that some music may be too *avante garde* when it is first played and that only over the years does it come to be revered. Culture largely determines what we find beautiful. For example, the definition of female beauty or male masculinity changes with the times. In the Victorian era a woman's naked ankle was considered beautiful and erotic. No more. Even within the same cultural moment, I may love Beethoven while you find Jimmy Hendrix awe inspiring. Many Americans find the game of soccer boring while many in Europe, South America, and elsewhere find in the game a sense of beauty that rivals that of ballet (and you may or may not find ballet an aesthetic experience).

The community of American antiques valued polished furniture for decades, only more recently valuing original painted surfaces. (The *Magazine Antiques* sends me to *The [London] Times* and an article that millennials are into brown antique furniture.) This same community at first admired weathervanes in near perfect condition only to redefine them as works of sculpture. In that redefinition bullet holes in the vanes became ancillary to shape, surface, and what the vane inspires in those looking at them.

Oftentimes those diagnosed with cancer become acutely aware of the here and now, espousing the idea that we should stop and smell the roses, that beauty is all around us if we will only slow down enough to perceive and appreciate it. The idea of Zen, that everyday tasks such as washing floors or cooking a meal, can be beautiful in their acts and simplicity brings aesthetic appreciation to the most mundane activities and moments in our lives. I find a perfectly shoveled sidewalk and driveway after a snowfall beautiful to behold as I lean on my shovel and look at the juxtaposition of the bare cement with the fresh snow covering the lawn. Crazy perhaps, but that is how I feel. Others feel the same way washing dishes by hand or pulling weeds in their garden.

I conclude that those who collect do so for one of, or a combination of many experiences, three of them being happiness, fulfillment, and aesthetic appreciation. Whatever collecting brings you, I hope you treasure the moments.

CHAPTER 2

Heart and Soul

From a religious perspective a soul is the immaterial or spiritual part of a person, his character or substance, often regarded as immortal. But the term has taken on different meanings over the years. Think of soul music, originating in the Black community in this country in the 1950s and 1960s, derived from gospel music and rhythm and blues, a hybrid of religious music and the secular, rock and roll sung gospel style. Here "soul" refers to an intensity, a depth, an emotional energy often presents in a work of art or music. The term "soul" for African Americans has connotations of pride in their identity and their culture. Soul music is marked by searing vocal intensity use of church-rooted call-and-response (such as Ray Charles "What'd I Say"), and a group of notes sung to one syllable.

Then there is soul food, also associated with African Americans in the southern United States (although its origins are more complex than this suggests). Given my heritage I consider chicken soup and a corned beef sandwich on rye to be soul food, and other ethnic groups also have foods they associate with their heritages. To oversimplify, soul food satisfies some deep (cynics would say primal) need or urge.

Regardless of the ethnic or cultural group these dishes hold deep cultural significance.

But soul has still another meaning as well, suited to our discussion of collectors. Collectors of American antiques, (or virtually any genre), make up a community. As a cultural group they may not have foods or music associated with other heritages, but they do have a bond and connection, an attachment to each other and their collecting enterprise that comes to define their core and ethos—their heart and soul. And as we all well know; many serious collectors give their heart and soul to their collecting. They share a pride in their identity and collecting culture. They would have stopped collecting years ago if this was not the case.

When we say someone is committed to something with their "heart and soul," we are tagging the depth of their commitment. They are not just casually involved, but fully invested emotionally, mentally, and sometimes even spiritually (if that term bothers you, consider that antiquarians "revere" the materials they collect—I will not mention Paul Revere, known for his silver).

That definition certainly encompasses me and other collectors I know. The agony of missing out on a piece I have searched for speaks to an emotional intensity that non-collectors might be hard put to understand. The fact that it does not take long when in casual conversation with someone for me to raise the fact that I collect American antiques speaks to how integral doing so is to my identity.

Collector Heart

When we say that someone has "heart," especially in the context of collectors, we are typically referring to their passion, dedication, and emotional investment in their collection. Their feelings are genuinely involved, and they care deeply about the outcome of their collecting. This emotional investment often drives them to persevere through challenges and setbacks because they are driven by a genuine love for what they are doing. Having heart means that the collector is deeply committed to her pursuit, driven by genuine enthusiasm and deep affection for the items she collects.

Collectors with heart do not just accumulate items for the sake of it; they genuinely care for and appreciate pieces in their collection and American antiques in general. Their emotional connected goes beyond mere material possession and adds depth and meaning to their collection and to their lives. This passion often shines through in their enthusiasm when discussing their collection or sharing stories about how they acquired certain items. Each antique may hold personal significance, evoke nostalgic memories, or represent a particular period or theme that resonates with them.

My passion is evidenced in the clock dial pictured. It sits in a Silas Hoadley (1786-1870) tallcase wooden works clock, the case average, pine painted black. But the dial in my mind is a "10" and is to die for. First is the eagle, sometimes found on Hoadley clocks. The eagle is Hoadley's last dial signature style from the early 1830s. But coupled with the eagle is a side wheeler paddle steamship of quite large dimension as it has a couple of decks. It flies an American flag.

We received information on the clock and dial from Ward Francillon in 1998 (he is now deceased), an expert on wooden works and Hoadley clocks. He did not recall ever seeing a vessel as depicted on the dial, another reason we love the clock. The image is rare or unique. I have only seen one other tallcase clock with an American flag and the flag coupled with the eagle takes my breath away. Perhaps to some, a bit crazy, but that is what makes collecting what it is.

Commitment and passion are certainly true for me, even for pieces I have added to our collection in recent years. Collectors mark the passing of time by the act of collecting. New to our collection are three Hudson Valley paintings. Despite their relative recent addition to our home, I regard them highly, equal to the admiration I hold for antiques we have lived with for far longer.

While some people may talk about their latest trip to Ireland or Seattle with fervor and photographs, serious collectors with heart also have wonderful stories related to their collecting. A recent one for me was visiting the Chipstone Foundation outside Milwaukee where I was able to view the best of

American antiques. Chipstone began with the collecting of Stanley and Polly Stone and is now dedicated to promoting scholarship of American decorative arts. It supports projects and publications at other institutions and is known for its support of scholarly works. It partners with the Milwaukee Art Museum, allowing many pieces in the Stone's collection to be viewed and appreciated by others.

I was there to pick up the highchair pictured in Chapter 8 that I had purchased in New Hampshire. It was delivered to Chipstone. I was appreciative of the hospitality I received. The director, Jon Prown, gave me a tour and invited me back. Oh, the antiques I saw. Perhaps only collectors with heart will understand but my visit was very special, one of the highlights of the year.

Collector Soul

To speak of a collector's soul signifies a deeper level of commitment beyond just emotion or persistence; it involves the essence of a person's being. A collector's very identity and values are intertwined with the cause or endeavor he is dedicated to. It suggests a profound alignment between his beliefs, principles, and the actions he takes. It touches on the collector's intensity, depth, and emotional energy as he goes about his collecting.

I cannot count the hours I have spent collecting nor would I probably want to. Decades ago, *Maine Antique Digest* had a monthly contest. It featured a close-up photograph of one segment of an antique pictured somewhere in that month's publication. The first person or first few persons (I forget which) to identify the piece received a *MAD* mug. I can remember the hours and hours I spent poring over *MAD* issues and think I still have two or three mugs put away somewhere. Who spends time doing something like that? A collector does and enjoys doing so. I certainly did.

An even better story was told to me by a dealer. His wife and young son accompanied him to the 2015 Connecticut Spring Antiques Show. Jonathan Rickard gave a ceramics "tour" of the show, leading a small group of attendees around the floor and making stops at different booths to discuss pots. The dealer's wife, with little interest in antiques took the "tour." A black basalt coffee pot caught her eye, and she liked it, an easy purchase decision. The coffee pot has been present in their house ever since, now prominently displayed in a cubby hole that reminds the dealer of a shelf he painstakingly built around the dozen or so pieces of "mocha" he took to the NHADA show around the same time they bought the coffee pot. Jonathan, a dealer they really liked, thought the shelves were great. The dealer and his wife did not see him often, but their interactions stand out vividly in his mind from the ten-year blur of show dealer life. The Black Basalt Coffee Pot transports this dealer to a moment in time, a dot in space on several different timelines—family life, show dealing, Jonathan. It has become part of this dealer's soul, or maybe a little part of his soul is attached to it.

Together, committing with both heart and soul creates a powerful synergy. It means that a collector is not just going through the motions or fulfilling obligations but is actively engaged and invested in his pursuits. Such collectors bring their entire being to the table, fostering a sense of authenticity, purpose, and resilience. This level of dedication often leads to profound personal growth and fulfillment, and a sense of place in the American antique community.

Did my collecting of American antiques over the decades lead to personal growth? Cognitive dissonance would argue it does. Who would want to look back and go "meh, it was just something to pass the time." Yet I do not believe I am engaging in psychological machinations to justify my collecting. I know I have learned patience, research skills, a respect, appreciation, and affection for people very different from myself, and an admiration for material culture and history I never would have developed otherwise.

Not to be exclusively focused on collectors I believe that many dealers also have heart and soul. While economically it could be argued they are finding and selling widgets I would disagree with this financial description. As one dealer told me, "There is pride, joy, and love."

I struggle with the question of when a collector knows that collecting has become part of his heart and soul. As I look back, there is no defining moment or moments I can point to that made American antiques an essential and fundamental part of me. It seemed to have developed gradually until it became an integral part of who I am. I would be interested in other collectors' insights into the matter.

In 1966 the Righteous Brothers released the song (You're My) *Soul and Inspiration.*

> (You're My) Soul and Inspiration. You're my
>   soul and my heart's inspiration
> Without you, baby, what good am I?
> I never had much going
> But at least I had you
> How can you walk out knowing
> I ain't got nothing left if you do, baby?
>
> You're my soul and my heart's inspiration
> Without you, baby, what good am I?
> Oh, what good am I?

Serious collectors of American antiques have no difficulty whatsoever identifying with "What good am I?" The devotion that is so much a part of them and the central place of collecting in their lives (their souls) is such that if collecting, for some reason, was denied to them, they would be lost and unmoored. Collecting is truly their soul and heart's inspiration. To borrow from Virginia Woolf, American antiques are the mirrors of these collectors' souls.

CHAPTER 3

Satisficers and Maximizers

A collector, it could be you, stands in line awaiting the opening of an American antique show with a wide variety of genres for sale. The magic hour arrives, and he enters, doing a quick walk-through and then more slowly examines the contents of dealers' booths. He sees some nice blanket chests, good paint, original surface. They are better than the ones that sit at the end of the beds in his home and would be a nice addition to his collection. Yet he keeps on walking. Then he pauses, a fine chest of drawers whispers to him, "come hither." And hither he goes. He is sorely tempted. Again, the chest is better than one he owns. He will consider it.

Pictured here is an acceptable blanket chest in the simple high-country aesthetic. The hue is darker than the very desirable robin's egg blue but still pretty. It has had a bit of work done to it. The painted surface shows its years. The surface is softer and more worn than it appears in the photo. It has nice moldings, height to its legs and cutout on the side. The blue matches the rope bed in the same bedroom; the similarity in color is an accident, not by design. A blanket chest such as this one would not be difficult to replace with a similar piece. Better blanket chests exist—Pennsylvania with wonderful hearts and flowers are just one example. Such chests are available on the market and affordable to us. But my wife and I are satisficers when it comes to this genre. We have lived with it for over 40 years and will continue to do so.

What is going on? The blanket chests do not draw more than a break in his step, but the chest of drawers brings him to a complete stop. Perhaps, like many collectors, he does not feel the urge to upgrade every genre in his collection. Satisficers, as I think of them, live with what they have, the stories behind them are worth telling; they are good enough. But in some genres collectors constantly seek better pieces. They may have owned several of a kind, each one reflecting heightened connoisseurship, and often an emptier wallet.

One explanation for this aspect of collector behavior is to draw a distinction between people who are labeled "satisficers" and those categorized as "maximizers" (the terms first appeared in 1956, proposed by the Nobel prize winner Herbert Simon), fancy words but ones that deepen our understanding of the collectors' experience. Simply put, maximizers are those collectors who want the very best. They seek superlative pieces and leave no stone unturned to find them. Maximizers are defined by their high standards, exhaustive and relentless searches, and oftentimes difficulty in making decisions. As one might expect a maximizing style has been associated with perfectionism.

Satisficers on the other hand are collectors for whom "good enough" is, well, good enough. Their criteria for what pieces are satisfactory tend to be modest instead of aspirational. Satisficers are no less demanding when they first purchase an antique nor less involved or interesting in the act of collecting. For most genres a piece other than superb quality, but still functional and perhaps a "looker" serves their needs. Perhaps familiarity or even a concession that imperfection (evidence of material culture) is also character plays a part in their collecting. Perhaps they are more sentimental and like and want to spend time with their "old friends" (see Chapter 26).

Maximizers may be perfectionists, but they also may simply orient to discernment. I have known people like that. They can see a scratch in a classic Rolls Royce and suddenly it is not that God-created object they had hoped for and passionately sought. The satisficer can bypass wonderful, affordable pieces because of a lack of interest. The ones at home bring pleasure enough.

In brief, both terms reflect what fulfills collectors' needs, how they approach the world of antiques and how they make decisions. I concede that a collector can be both a satisficer and a maximizer, finding his blanket chests "good enough" but wanting the best in chests of drawers.

Both satisficers and maximizers or whichever genre elicits maximizing or satisfying behaviors, find their decisions prudent and wise. Often, they simply shrug their shoulders, struggling to understand and verbalize why that average bedside stands have never been upgraded (which is true of Sandy and me), but the chest of drawers is far from the first. Each style motivates behavior, either to purchase or not, to be interested and invested, or not. Passing by the blanket chests leads to no feelings of regret. Not considering or buying the chest of drawers may niggle for months to come. Of course, such decision making and collecting styles can drive dealers crazy.

I have seen bedside stands with better paint or more delicate legs. Yet I am not motivated as a collector to upgrade. Why my criteria for these stands are modest is a mystery to me. But for this genre of American antiques, the status quo suffices. But I am driven to upgrade the paintings in our collection, weathervanes, and as noted, chests of drawers. A collector's maximizing or satisfaction has nothing to do with money. For some genres, a small fortune may be spent on a small painted Shaker box. In another genre, much less money has purchased a very visible piece of case furniture a collector has lived with for years. Spend more here, "yes, I must."

The goals of a maximizer are loftier than a satisficer,

sometimes unachievable. The maximizer holds a lantern that lights his path as he searches for the perfect antique. The lantern's light is everlasting. Looking for the perfect MacGuffin can be a lifelong task, and the work that goes into finding pieces that maximizer collectors are pleased with can become an obsession, both an exhaustive and exhausting process.

Maximizers as you may have guessed are more likely to suffer from collectors' buyer's remorse. "Is this piece the best I can find?" "Perhaps there is something better out there?" They may even feel anticipatory regret for the hunt is never ending for better and best. Paradoxically, satisficers may be more content with the pieces in their collection, even though maximizers may develop superior collections over time. Satisficers appreciate their antiques for what they are with no inner drive seeking perfection (or at least better). Maximizers are often the collectors of Americana whose collections are extolled (if they are wealthy and can afford the best and their connoisseurship developed and superb). But both maximizers and satisficers can collect mid-market pieces. It is the maximizer who may find himself, however, moving from mid-market to the *crème de la crème*. To some the drive for the best may seem at times like a curse.

How people become maximizers or satisficers is unknown. Perhaps genetics play a role, emphasizing a need for order, or accentuating compulsive behaviors. Satisficers may be more "laid back," again genetics may play a role in each personality style. I cannot rule out what was rewarded when a future collector was a child or teen, or what the parents modeled if they themselves collected. All may play a role. Sigmund Freud once said, "A man should not strive to eliminate his complexes but to get into accord with them: They are legitimately what directs his conduct in the world." I suspect that maximizers and satisficers are doing just that.

None the less, one can learn to be a maximizer, and one also can learn to be a satisficer, at least in some areas of collecting. The values of and lessons dealers have taught with whom collectors work, for example, may educate a collector early on to appreciate only the best. At the same time the canard, "buy the best you can afford" may not apply to all genres of American antiques according to fellow collectors or dealers. An average piece made 20 miles from where the collector lives in the Connecticut Valley may have more attraction than a superb piece made by a craftsman who worked much further away. Connoisseurship may flourish in one genre but not another. The former requires looking for the best, the latter does not.

Of course, the road to which genres a collector falls in love with is foggy and ill defined. When my wife and I first began collecting I do not believe anyone could have predicted what we now love, and which pieces despite our years of collecting we would like to upgrade (a maximizing style), and which are good enough. If we upgrade, we are maximizers as there is no point in doing so unless we purchase the very best.

Collectors are well advised to enjoy the mysteries of why they collect what they do and how they go about it. As a collector I have no idea as to why certain genres lead to Sisyphus like behavior—continually looking for a better example of "x" or "y," finding it, and then pushing the boulder (antique) back up the hill by looking still more. Mysteries add robustness and richness to collecting. Were I to learn why I am a satisficer when it comes to blanket chests, the insight would be relatively worthless. In this case I like leaving the unknown, unknown. The maximizer in me has work to do. I would like to find a wonderful kettle stand in original surface with its small top, for example.

Maximizers are forced to live with, and hopefully enjoy, the aphorism that perfection is the enemy of the good. In fact, most do not see their quests for better pieces as untoward but rather as part and parcel of the collector's world. They live for the moment an antique takes their breath away, and when it does, the feeling and moment rewards all their energy, time, and dollars seeking perfection. With so many Americana genres to choose from, their journeys can be never ending, collecting a lifetime endeavor.

The satisficer, not so much. As their home (s) fill, they view their collection with pleasure. If only one or two genres motivate maximizer behavior, they may find that "perfect" piece in their estimation and be satisfied with it. They often find a level of contentment and pleasure in their antiques that a maximizer can only wish for.

Which collector makes the better decision you might ask? While many expect it to be the maximizer who uses a great deal of information in making his decisions to maximize future benefit it is the satisficer, who uses more modest criteria, who, surprisingly, makes better decisions. Maximizers suffer under high self-expectations while satisficers feel none of this pressure. Maximizers often struggle with unachievable goals, satisficers merely want to be *satisfied*.

In other words, "Done is better than perfect" (unknown) encapsulates the satisficer approach to collecting. A maximizer would be horrified. For the latter, Oscar Wilde captures the essence of collecting, "It is through art, and through art only, that we can realize our perfection." Regardless of which style captures your collector essence, both types of collectors preserve history in the American antiques they seek and enjoy every day. Happy satisficing and maximizing in your collecting in the days ahead.

CHAPTER 4
Personalities and Collecting

Who we are affects what and how we collect. That is a given, but how are we to understand the relationship between one and the other, ourselves and our collections? Theorists have proposed many taxonomies to define, measure, and encompass personality. Let's use the "big five" (supported by research) in understanding those who collect Americana. This scheme says we should consider five personality characteristics in understanding people's (and in our case collectors' behaviors): extroversion (versus introversion), agreeableness (versus criticalness), openness (versus consistency and cautiousness), conscientiousness, (versus extravagance) and neuroticism (versus confidence).

The Neurotic Collector

Calvin reached out to his favorite dealers once again. Was the paint on the Windsor chair as represented? Was the painted box period and not a reproduction? He had a nice collection, but he overthinks his purchases, agonizing over every acquisition. Insecurity is his calling card, doubting his middle name. Oh, he worries to his detriment, sticking to safer options has limited the breadth and depth of his collection, which as a result he little enjoys. Like many collectors he does research but more so to validate his choices and alleviate his anxiety than to refine his practice and possessions. Calvin needs a lot of dealer reassurance and hand holding.

The Confident Collector

John approaches the antique show with self-assuredness and conviction. If he sees something to add to his collection he buys it, no dithering. After all, he who hesitates is lost. As he approaches a dealer whom he knows with questions about a piece, he is assertive in negotiating the price. John likes sharing his passion with others in line before the show opens. He remains steadfast in his convictions and preferences, despite criticism or feedback that differs from his beliefs. At times he can be prickly to be around, but he revels in his collecting triumphs.

The Extroverted Collector

I suspect just about everyone has met Abagail, the overly friendly (and maybe overly verbal) collector. Abagail is outgoing, sociable and energetic, collecting bold and expressive objects or at least less than safe ones. If you meet her in line before a show opens, she'll pull you into the history of what she collects and show you photos of her collection. While she is a delight, she also makes people nervous: as she never appears to lack for opinions which she fiercely, loudly and constantly expresses. But if you listen closely, she is well-read and expert in her chosen field.

The Solidary and Reserved Collector

Andrew is known to have quite a superb collection of Americana, and he is asked about it often. But his is a private enjoyment. He finds fulfillment in the quiet, solitary moments he spends living with it. His approach to collecting mirrored his personality and research—deep reflection and contemplation, a thoughtful and introspective mindset. Andrew does not flee all social engagements but is selective with whom he interacts. He prefers smaller, intimate gatherings or one-on-one conversations with like-minded individuals. You will find Andrew at an antique show at a table where lunch wraps and sandwiches are sold, either alone or talking earnestly with one other collector. Andrew makes discerning choices, is highly selective in his acquisitions, carefully considering each piece before adding it to his collection. He values quality over quantity, opting for pieces that resonate deeply with him on a personal level. Once dealers get to know Andrew they enjoy talking and working with him. They know that coupled with his reserved demeanor is a connoisseur.

The Agreeable Collector

Theodore is well respected and liked in the American antique world. He is a friendly and compassionate person who dealers enjoy (wishing secretly that more collectors could be like him.) Like the confident collector, Theodore takes pleasure in sharing his knowledge and time, but simply because he likes other people, not out of pride in what he has accomplished. At an antique show or when visiting a dealer's shop, he might ask once, "is that the best you can do?" and then accept the dealer's price. His consideration for others, including his sensitivity to how hard dealers work and their need to make a living, is his calling card. He values his personal connections as much as the antiques themselves, fostering a sense of community and belonging within the Americana world.

This early child's eastern Connecticut or Rhode Island chair was purchased from well-known dealers and in this case, I was an agreeable collector. Sandy and I love the chair, especially its surface. We smile at the flattened front posts from the many times the chair was pushed over, and a toddler held onto it as he learned to walk. I asked the dealer the "best he could do" and agreed to the price he asked. The price was fair, and I saw no reason to dicker. As is often said, "go find another one." A chair like this does not come onto the market often. "Why strain a good relationship (by trying to save a few dollars)?" is one of my collecting maxims and in my thinking when the chair was acquired. Since then, we have purchased from this dealer again.

The Critical Collector

Harry catches sight of a small weathervane in a dealer's booth at a show. He looks at it from a distance, then approaches. It talks to him. Harry, like many collectors has a keen eye for quality and authenticity. The weathervane is a fine example: Its surface and small size make it a winner. Harry's discerning taste, he is also a connoisseur, ensures that his collection maintains a high standard of excellence. But Harry, unlike Theodore, is not a dream for dealers to work with. His quest for perfection and constantly seeking out the best examples within his chosen genres mean his exacting standards become a liability, as he is most often not satisfied. His critical style leads him to invest significant time and effort in researching and acquiring top-tier pieces. This pursuit of perfection (not anxiety) drives him to continually refine his collection.

Typically, the critical collector—our Harry—is not afraid to offer honest and constructive feedback to others. His critical perspective often provides valuable insights and contributes to the growth and development of the American antique community but can be a bitter pill to swallow. Sometimes he does not balance his knowledge and critiques with diplomacy and tact, inadvertently alienating dealers or fellow collectors.

The Open Collector

Nancy approaches collecting as she does most things in life, with enthusiasm and a sense of exploration. She is driven to study diverse styles and genres. Dealers do not know what will catch her eye as she seems to eagerly try a wide range of artistic styles, and periods, embracing diversity in her collection. She is drawn to unusual, pieces that challenge traditional norms, on the prowl for the next cutting edge "thing."

But Nancy is no fly-by-night collector. Hers is an undertaking with constant learning and discovery as she seeks to expand her knowledge and understanding. Her research allows her to make more informed collecting decisions and develop a deeper appreciation for her collection. Experimentation and risk-taking are her middle names as she embraces the unknown or little known. Dealers with similar tastes like working with her. She is kind in sharing what she learns with others in the Americana community leading to several articles in trade publications.

The Consistent and Cautious Collector

Jimmy, like Andrew, approaches collecting with a more methodical and deliberate mindset. He is a disciplined collector. Reliable is his middle name. Dealers always know what he is looking for as he has a list in his pocket. He wants a reminder of his vision for his collection and will not be dissuaded from his collecting goals and focus. In Jimmy's case he focuses on Connecticut River Valley antiques, Queen Anne or slightly later, carefully curating his acquisitions. Like collectors with other personality styles, Jimmy does thorough research and due diligence. He is most comfortable with a cohesive collection, not merely Connecticut Valley but striving for coherence and consistency, carefully selecting pieces that complement each other aesthetically. Jimmy has all the patience in the world, willing to wait for the right opportunities and exercises restraint when necessary.

The Conscientiousness Collector

George exemplifies the trait itself. Like Jimmy, he is described by dealers as an efficient and organized collector. He would be horrified to be described as extravagant or careless.

Once again, his style is methodical. He walks the antique show floor again and again, comparing pieces displayed with a focus on his collection. This meticulous approach helps George make informed decisions and track the evolution of his collection over time, aided as one would expect by careful research. Strategic planning is George's middle name. He knows what key pieces will fill gaps in his collection and advance its quality, and his satisfaction with it. But he is not averse to pieces from different locales, big city or high-country, miniature portraits or full-sized.

The Extravagant Collector

Richard on the other hand is comfortable with making impulsive and spontaneous purchases. His decisions seem totally hasty and reckless but are driven by his immediate aesthetic or emotional response to pieces. He is drawn to the flashy or extravagant that make a bold statement. People like Richard give collecting its fizz. Not for them the traditional Paul Revere silver; the *fraktur* of the Pennsylvania Dutch, the perfect 1890 silver dollar. Richard also places a high value on the status and prestige associated with owning rare antiques and paintings, regardless of practical considerations such as provenance or historical significance. "In your face" is Richard's middle name. He loves provoking reactions in fellow collectors. Surprisingly, but not to Richard, while less organized in his approach to collecting than many others, he pays meticulous attention to the presentation and display of his collection.

Richard, like most other extravagant collectors likes to experiment with pieces that push the boundaries of traditional tastes and aesthetics. He enjoys the thrill of discovery and novelty, although collectors with more Catholic tastes in American antiques are often horrified at what he purchases.

And where am I as a collector—a bit more anxious than

confident, extroverted than introverted, agreeable than criti-cal, consistent and cautious than open, and conscientious, not extravagant. Have these traits influenced our collection? They have. For example, I can remember several pieces I "should" have purchased but did not, because of being cautious.

The five personality traits do overlap, none is pure unto itself. But hopefully the discussion, while not conclusive offers insights into readers' and others' collecting behaviors. It did so for me. Many collector approaches to collecting, influenced by their personality styles, have their merits, and the right one for an individual collector depends on his personal preferences, values, and objectives. But collectors can pick out traits that apply to them and ask themselves how these personality traits affect the enjoyment quality and nature of their collecting and collection.

CHAPTER 5

Resilience

Collecting has its moments, both good and painful. As such, it is a microcosm of our lives. Collectors cherish the good times, the finds, the successes, the wins. But they also must endure the losses, the "almosts," the emptiness, the defeats, the need to adjust, rediscover their equilibrium, and carry on. As described in Chapter 8, the hunt does go awry and because of that collecting takes resilience—the ability to spring back and recover from difficulties. Collectors need toughness.

Recently I saw a painting in an advertisement in *Maine Antique Digest*, only a half hour after that issue went "live" online. How it stirred the embers of my anticipation. I loved it, and I do not easily fall in love. I immediately called the dealer in question and learned it had sold a few days previously. Would its availability been too much to ask? Would it have been too much trouble to be able to purchase it? Apparently so. To say I was disappointed is an understatement. My feelings were much more intense than mere disappointment.

Collecting is not always pleasant, and my feelings got me thinking about gut-wrenching moments in collecting, when my little world reeked of injustice, and the staid, predictable collectors' universes had suddenly become unhinged. But like many collectors I carried on.

A friend asked me if my feelings on this occasion were more severe than losing out on an antique I coveted at auction "Yes," the feeling was more intense as I never really had a shot at owning the painting. I will not enumerate all the ways and all the situations in which collectors can be disappointed. Any seasoned collector I am sure is aware of most or all of them and would add to the list.

When collectors' expectations, hopes and desires are thwarted, life darkens—feelings of disappointment, anger, chagrin, sadness, resentment, discouragement, and perhaps for some collectors the milder feeling *nonplussed* grip at the gut, fill the mind, touch the heart. I was miserable, suffering from the loss, for I naively expected the painting to still be on the market. My expectations were high, and the higher they are the further a collector falls if they are unmet.

I admit in retrospect that these reactions sound and even feel over-the-top, but at that moment they were real enough. Massive disappointment is rare in my life, but here it was, peeking through the pages of my favorite journal, now conspicuously and figuratively stamped "Not for You" in bold red letters.

Yes, I know that the lead time for such an ad can be weeks, that the dealer in question had a shop, and that most dealers would be spreading the word about a special piece long before the ad appeared. But nonetheless ... the suffering was real, not physical pain but emotional anguish. Unrequited love comes to mind. It is an affliction I have experienced before as a collector and no doubt will again. I do not believe in an American antique goddess who metes out lessons and justice. But if I did, she was punishing me on this occasion.

Some collectors, wiser than I, might have entered the scenario by immediately lowering their expectations. "Perhaps the painting will still be on the market." "Perhaps I will get lucky this time." I did no such thing and was hit full bore by my feelings of loss. Of course, lowering expectations also lowers hope, enthusiasm, passion, and what makes collecting such a driving force for collectors. In for a penny, in for a pound the saying goes. I was fully submerged.

Other situations come to mind when collectors may enter the "dark side" of emotions that they need to fight through to emerge in the sunlight once again. If collectors' preferences, that is, their right to have their own tastes and choices are confronted, they are likely to become upset. "Who is this other person (e.g., fellow collector, dealer) to pass judgment on me?" While an experienced collector always wants to learn more and is eager to do so, such learning if too confrontive can be off putting. Of course, the interaction may not be about learning at all. Someone else might simply have been insensitive or enjoys winding other collectors up to see how they respond.

It becomes clear why my feelings were more intense and "negative" about this painting than failing at auction or shows, for example. I know that at auctions others may have deeper pockets than I, no matter how deep I want to financially reach. And shows can be a gamble. A collector chooses this aisle, another chooses a different aisle. Even if both are near the front of the line as the show opens, it is fate that both love the same genre and who gets the antique. Capturing the moment, it is easier for a collector to tell himself, "That's the way the cookie crumbles."

I can say that self-talk is a good way to cope with dis-appointment, loss or clenching one's fist at an unfair world but it would be fatuous to say that it is a tried-and-true salve to what collectors feel. "Maybe next time." "You win some you lose some." "Success is 95% showing up and persistence." "When life gives you lemons, make lemonade." All of these are examples of positive self-talk. But the downside of being an older collector is that time is running out. So, I will not, even though I know research supports such self-talk at helping collectors cope, propose the mechanism as a panacea. Such self-talk certainly did not work for me in this instance. My response was "bah!"

Collectors also can feel let down by others and themselves. The auctioneer misses your bid or even at an on-line auction awards the piece to someone else. The dealer does not save the piece for you as he said. The list could go on and on. "Would it be asking too much of someone else or ourselves?" Again, apparently so.

Letting ourselves down may be the worse as there is no place to hide when this occurs. Had I not called about the painting I probably would have been even more upset with myself. "All it took was a phone call. Why didn't you call?" "Dummy. Mutter, mutter." I am talking once again about expectations, but expectations in ourselves. When collectors fail to live up to their own standards of behavior, they kick themselves or worse.

If there was any upside to my feelings about the painting, it was that I knew I still had fire in my belly as a collector. A good collector needs such resilience. The hunt goes on after all. It was positive that I was still able to fall in love with a piece. "Small consolation" I told myself, but a consolation, nonetheless. That is one important purpose of dismay. If collectors listen to themselves, they become aware of what it is they expect from others, themselves, and the world. This self-awareness is important for collector. As they assess the situations in which life has ceased to be a bowl of cherries, and share them with others, they learn whether their expectations and responses are realistic, as neither need be.

The painting's unavailability (to me) reminded me of another valuable lesson as a collector. Loving antiques and losing out on them exist on a continuum. The more a collector loves, just as with the higher a collector's expectations, the more intense the feelings when life smacks him around (again). A third lesson comes to mind: The feelings abated after a week or two. I found the collecting air sweet once again. I just had to endure my disappointment. I returned to my collecting routine.

Collectors need resilience, the ability to carry on, to adapt to difficult circumstances, to bleakness. That how the movie *Gone with The Wind* ends. Scarlett O'Hara tells herself, "For after all, tomorrow is another day!" Resilience theory posits that it is not the seriousness of the adversity we face that is critical but how we respond to it. Resilience enables us to cope and move forward. For life, and as any collector knows, collecting is never perfect. Frustrations and misfortunes must be dealt with. We must continue or learn to collect in a healthy, productive manner. Pouting, whining, giving up, curling into the fetal position, drinking too much, becoming depressed or angry; these are all possible responses.

The folk-art painting pictured, *Black to Move* is wonderful in our opinion, and my wife and I love it. It adds to her collection of Black memorabilia. When we saw it, we already owned a print from the June 4, 1881, issue of *Harper's Weekly* (page 360) titled, *A Lesson in History-Decoration Day* (drawn by S. G. McCutcheon). The black and white drawing depicts an aging Black man sitting on a tombstone in a cemetery talking to several Black children. One assumes he served in the civil war but that is supposition on our part. We liked this image very much and had not seen another for sale. When it arrived, however, it had been damaged in shipping. We persevered and found a restorer out east who did a wonderful job. When it returned, we were pleased to say the least. Decoration Day was to become Memorial Day, the name harkens to the idea of honoring the war's dead by decorating the graves of Union soldiers.

We looked for other images with elder Blacks and children. One painting was far too expensive, otherwise there was nothing on the market we came across for years. However, we did not give up. And then the above pictured painting was in a dealer's booth. We pounced on it, releasing our disappointment and reveling in the new find.

Resilience differs collector to collector, depending on their backgrounds, goals, and present life situations. A difficult setback for a neophyte collector may end the hobby; it is simply not fun he concludes. For an experienced collector it may take a series of adversities to really knock him off kilter, although not necessarily. In other words, there is no one best series of behaviors that define collector resilience. The question is what is the specific set of responses that is a best fit for each collector who needs to take a deep breath, weather the storm, and continue collecting.

Some collectors may share their dilemmas with others who have experienced the same disappointments, finding that simply doing that rights the ship. And they may get good advice in the process. Other collectors may let their feelings come to the surface, knowing it may be painful for a while but that "this too shall pass." For still others long walks or turning their attention to other matters helps a return to equilibrium. To each their own.

The best collectors have a gambler's mentality: Being thrilled and disappointed are equally possible, but there is something indefinable—though frequently dissected in this book—that drives them to keep searching. The ideal is out there somewhere. Maybe we can find it.

I hope I have convinced the reader that all collectors need such "resilient toughness." For losses and mistakes are a certainty in the collecting world. They truthfully tell themselves that other antiques will come to them that they want to add to their collections. Few things in collecting are permanent or beyond recovery. Collecting may be a metaphorical disease, but it is not fatal.

As for me, I shall persevere, aware that in many ways I had created my own suffering. My desires were strong and went unfulfilled. Lyndon B. Johnson was correct. "Yesterday is not ours to recover, but tomorrow is ours to win or lose." Or the day after tomorrow or the day after that, as any collector knows. For suffering is unavoidable if one collects. The trick is not wallowing in it for too long. Collectors may not know how they pull themselves back from the abyss of negative emotion, but they manage to do so. So as the 1936 song says (composed by Jerome Kern),

> Pick yourself up
> Take a deep breath
> Dust yourself off
> And start all over again

For that is what collectors do. A solid collector is someone with coping mechanisms, a strong sense of realism, and the realization that the collector's world is, in fact, the same dog-eat-dog universe that life is. What is important is that the collector—who does not have destiny in his hands has two things going for him: a well-deep knowledge of those genres of Americana he has researched and the understanding that his subject is infinite. For every discouragement in collecting, there is a balancing moment of elation and that is why people (some people) indulge. As for now, while collecting does not always go smoothly or well, it is all collectors have. And collectors must collect, if for no other reason that is who they are, enjoying the pursuit and ownership of beautiful objects while they can.

CHAPTER 6

Wonderings

After listening to collectors for a long, long time, I have concluded that they wonder about things a great deal. There is a lot going on in collectors' heads related to their collecting and collections. They ponder, they speculate, reflect, ask themselves questions, puzzle about and meditate on a great deal of collecting business. They are curious to the point of exhaustion. You would think a collector's head would explode at some point.

I recently consigned a few pieces to a dealer. One reason was that my wife and I had upgraded our horse-and-sulky weathervane (pictured in Chapter 24) after some years, and it came with a great story to boot. Shipping the items to New England would have been prohibitive given their lesser value so I found a dealer in Wisconsin. I told him there was no hurry in getting back to me. I was successful in getting them out of the house, so my mission was half completed.

And I wondered: "How will they be sold—auction, passed on to another dealer, from a website? What will they bring?" Although if I could take my wife out for a good dinner or two, I would be happy. "How long will it take before I hear from the dealer?" Trust is an interesting interpersonal commodity, and I trust this dealer, although it may be quite some time before he moves forward. So, I wondered.

A great deal of wondering takes place in the line collectors form before a show. One couple talked of looking for baskets that had to be perfect and painted. Would they find any? They did and were thrilled about that. Would a favored dealer have a piece newly unveiled to the world another collector could not live without? I have purchased several Black dolls for my wife's collection from a dealer at the New Hampshire Dealers Show. She tells me she will have one in her booth but does not want to send photos beforehand. I tell her that I understand so that it truly is fresh to the market and wonder if it will meet my wife's criterion—would she have loved it as a child? As it turned out she would not have, so we passed.

If I fall in love with a piece, will my wife like it enough to give me the green light to purchase it? I remember once we traded—a weathervane for me and a piece of jewelry for her. She has a better eye than I for displaying our collection and puts the brakes on my emotions when the house begins to get too cluttered. Those phone calls to her in Wisconsin, after I have emailed a picture or two from New England of a piece that I covet, are full of the unknown. I wonder what she will say.

Of course, collectors are not the only ones in the American antique universe who do a lot of wondering. Look at wonderings from a dealer's perspective. "Will the show be a good one, marked by good buying and selling, and follow-up sales as well?" "Will I sell to a collector new to me and perhaps develop a relationship that leads to more sales?" "Will the stock market behave itself and not tank a few days before the show opens?" "Will the world cooperate with no new wars or bad news casting a pall over everyone and everything?"

On occasion I have asked a dealer to bring a piece from an advertisement or his website to a show so I can see it in person. I always wonder if it will look the same, better, or worse? One watercolor painting was too dark for my tastes, although I very much like the scene it depicted, Mt. Vernon to be exact. Another pair of ship paintings were wonderful but well beyond my budget. I can wonder (perhaps hope) that I will fall in love with the piece (I have written about Hope in *The Collector's World*), but I have learned to wait and let the moment be my guide.

The opposite of asking a dealer to bring a piece a collector has seen pictures and descriptions of, is finding an antique in a dealer's booth fresh to the market and unavailable until the prospective buyer enters the booth. Before a show I always wonder if that will happen to me. There are several pieces in our collection that meet this criterion, and it is an exciting moment in our collectors' hunt—a Black doll, my wife's second at that point in time (pictured in *Come Collect with Me*), a blanket chest (also pictured in *Come Collect with Me*), a Chambers painting (pictured in Chapter 7), and other pieces in our collection have satisfied this wondering for us.

Collectors do a lot of wondering about what a piece will bring. Whether one of their own or a piece at auction, collectors often set benchmarks in their heads based on their personal estimate of what is an acceptable price. Will I feel okay my painted boxes brought "x?" Will I bid if the piece at auction rises to "y?" When looking at pieces in booths, shops, and online collectors also wonder how firm the price is. Will the dealer come down so I can both afford the antique and feel good about purchasing it? Where is the market heading? Will I end up with a nice grouping of antiques that proved to be a fad, or will its desirability endure?

Then there is the wondering of time. How long will a collector search for a piece of painted furniture, weathervane, painting and the like to upgrade her collection? Sometimes it feels like forever (and a day). And then at a show the antique goddess (to whom I do not worship but probably should) is most unfair—the collector finds two desirable ones in the same genre. Which one to purchase? she wonders. Both may have attributes that meet the collector's connoisseurship criteria, either would have been acceptable. Someone accompanying the collector may wonder, which will she choose and why?

When a collector divorces his collection (see Chapter 29), the world is full of wondering. Did I make the correct choice in how I went about it? Should I have consigned more pieces to dealer "x"? Should I have broken the collection up and used multiple auction houses? Did I clearly make my wishes known? Did I take enough time in making my decisions? Depending on the collector's personality the wondering can morph into obsessiveness and rumination. Typically, there is never enough data to firmly know that one has made the correct decision. Hunker down if one can and wait for the outcomes. But I wonder ... ? the collector asks herself.

Then there is the wondering that borders on lament as the collector bemoans and regrets decisions he has made. I wonder why I didn't bid once more at the auction just to see what would happen? Maybe I would have gotten lucky? I wonder why did I not allow myself to spend what the dealer was asking for the piece? I knew it was special. I wonder why I bought what I did? I wonder why I sold what I did, especially that one piece I wish I had back? I wonder if I am ever going to be a "good" collector? I wonder why I punish myself with wonderings such as these.

I wondered if I ever would find information about a young lady's folk-art painting of a view of the Hudson from West Point (see Chapter 14). The answer seems to be "No." I wondered about the craftsman who made a triple back Windsor we own with a seat I have never seen pictured in any of the superb books on this genre. (pictured in *Come Collect with Me*). The skeptic in me wonders if our stack of painted boxes contains one or two that are not original. There is no end to wondering.

We love *Boston Harbor from Across the Bay*. We lived with it for several years and then had it cleaned. The difference was remarkable with the sky blue and the details visible. When we purchased it, the dealer had someone look at it and tell us that he thought (but not definitively) that the artist was Robert Weir. We have continued to wonder if he is indeed the limner.

The painting has a plaque centered at bottom of painting on the frame that reads BOSTON HARBOR FROM ACROSS THE BAY 1827. It is an oil on canvas in its original frame. We were told the signature in the lower right corner, Robert w, matches Weir's signature and that the stylized trees are painted in his manner.

But I cannot find a listing of this painting among Weir's works.

Weir was an American artist and an instructor at the United States Military Academy (West Point). The date of the painting (although anyone can attach a plaque to a frame) fits his return from Europe.

As an author I hope that this book resonates with readers and perhaps changes a collecting behavior here and there. It did so for me. In thinking about this painting, I became motivated to roll up my sleeves and once and for all learn, if possible, who the artist truly is. I have reached out to a gallery in Boston, but they were not familiar enough with Weir's work to attempt an attribution. I now must find a "Weir expert." Wish me luck.

Collector wonderings can take the form of doubt, not necessarily bad but such self-questioning can be draining. Such thoughts in my experience occur more in the dead of winter, a good glass of port in hand. I wonder if the authenticity of the painted tin container is as described. I wonder if I really have kept up enough on the market. I wonder if I am taking good enough care of pieces in my collection. What could I do differently to maintain their condition and ensure their longevity? I wonder if my strategies to build my collection are valid and robust? I wonder if the insurance for my collection is adequate. At least the latter two wonderings can be validated by talking with other collectors and dealers. I wonder if I need to expand my relationships with collectors and dealers.

Also making use of that glass of port are the deeper wonderings, as I think of them. Of all the forms of beautiful objects and art why am I so interested in American history, its geography and craftsman and painters? Why American antiques? Why does evidence of the passage of time, the material culture these objects bear and bring with them fascinate me so? Why not collect American stamps, autos, or coins? Will I ever truly make sense of myself as a collector?

It could be that the more a collector knows about her collection, the more doubts she can have. The act of wondering may contribute to the pleasure (think of mathematicians thinking about math or authors thinking about plots) of collecting.

These are just some of the things that collectors ponder. Their mindsets are never static. Each of these themes (wonderings) provide a rich basis for exploring different aspect of a collector's demeanor, perspective, sentiments, and experience. I wonder if the intriguing thoughts and questions ever end. I think not.

CHAPTER 7

Awe

He who can no longer pause to wonder and stand rapt
in awe, is as good as dead; his eyes are closed.

Albert Einstein

How does one live the good life? This age-old question has no single definitive answer. But collectors of American antiques would respond, "Collecting, of course." Here I explore a feeling and experience that contributes to these collectors' good lives—awe.

Awe varies from person to person, just as beauty does, so what one collector finds awe-inspiring another may not. Typically, when people are awestruck, they say that things are larger, brighter, more dangerous, louder than they had ever imagined they could be (and the list can surely be added to), and the (awe inspiring) encounter took them aback: We were "awed," agape, baffled, frightened. Awe implies a deep feeling of reverence, for our purposes for the American antique being viewed, touched, and felt and sometimes owned.

A dealer posts a photo of a pair of wonderful Windsor chairs on social media. One collector comments: "I am in awe." The chairs are more than astounding, amazing, breathtaking, or stunning than he imagined they might or could be. The collector is experiencing something baffling, perhaps beyond what mere language can capture.

In many cases we have the possibility of awe hardwired into our brains. Being awed is an experience and emotion in the face of mysteries. It is the abyss between everyday experience and expectation, what I call brushes with the heavens. To the collector viewing the Windsor chairs, they truly were heaven-sent. This happened to a dealer I know once. When he first saw a New York State paint-decorated blanket chest in a collector's home some years ago, it had a beam of sunlight lighting up the front panel within a darkened room. The drama of the chest stunned him and quite literally took his breath away. The colors, the composition, the earliness—a masterpiece and his response, one of quiet reverence and awe.

Awe transforms the collector or dealer. In the presence of that antique, everyday quibbles disappear and The Awed (if I may use such a term) realizes he or she is in the presence of something special in life. Their up-to-then understanding of antiques is erased, distorted, or expanded. Awe supersedes the simple appreciation and apprehension of beauty. The collector recognizes that he is now part of something larger than himself or something else is part of him. He may feel small and insignificant in the presence of this antique and experience moments of inner peace.

I look at a Thomas Chambers' 1840 painting, *A View of the Hudson from West Point*. If you have ever seen the view in person, it is a treasure to behold, nature limned at its best by Chambers. Chambers, of whom little is known but much is conjectured has been "discovered." Any painting almost 200 years old in wonderful condition is awe-inspiring to me. I then look at a DeGrailly painting of the same scene painted 10 years later (pictured in Chapter 11). Again, a work in marvelous condition, painted by a more formally trained artist. Both painters captured this scene and painted it because they were captivated by it, and certainly the scene resonated with those who bought paintings so long ago, just as both resonate with me today.

The Chambers' painting is a wonderful piece of folk-art. The sailboats with their sails luffing while the water is smooth. The American flag flying from one of the boats. The use of colors. The work is in wonderful condition. Chambers has captured the view from West Point and interpreted it at the same time. The painting takes my breath away. I might add that it stands alone in our collection in eliciting wonderment from friends who visit. They look at the painting and their jaws drop. It has that effect on people.

A story, if I may. I am not alone in my affection for and response to Chambers' paintings of this scene. They do not last long on the market. I purchased the painting at a premier show of American antiques with a line of 500 people or more waiting to enter when the doors opened. The dealer from whom I purchased the painting typically does not let collectors place holds on pieces to make up their minds as the demand is high. I knew the dealer and had worked with him before and when I asked about a hold he gave me 10 minutes. When I returned to his booth someone else had his checkbook out, ready to buy the painting if I did not. The other collector also found the painting magical when I talked with him, albeit disappointed it could not be his.

How does one describe the feeling? Almost two centuries after someone looked at each of these works of art and wanted it in his home, I reached the same conclusion. Something about these two pictures captured an undefined, unmeasured depth that I had unconsciously within me. The two painters stroked not only my feeling but a sense that what they had done exceeded mere skill. We casually use the word "art," but we tend to forget that through history the term has variously been associated with the divine, the magical and the inspired. When an object reaches those levels, awe is the result, rare as it may be.

Awe is an intense emotional experience typically elicited by encountering something vast, beautiful, or extraordinary. Our ordinary expectations are thrown out, both confounded and exceeded, and our experience is expanded. Thus, natural phenomena are one such trigger—the power of mother nature through a storm, volcano, or blizzard; a sky full of stars or the northern lights; or the unexpected grandeur of the Hudson. We may be humbled by the realization of how small we are amid such a vast environment, connected to our ancestors from ages ago and removed for the moment from the world in which we live.

Awe also can be triggered by artistic creations of a different sort. I think of Beethoven's 9th symphony, in and of itself a *tour de force* but even more awe inspiring when one realizes he composed the opus while deaf. Genius at work. Michelangelo's David and the Sistine Chapel ceiling are other examples. To many it is impossible that something so beautiful had been created by an artist's hands.

Any collector of American antiques knows that when in the presence of an exceptional craftsman's work, a feeling of awe often accompanies the experience—its beauty, its timelessness, the skill it took to create it (whether in its simplicity or not). The fact that it survived so long given its fragility, rarity, or circumstances of war may contribute to the feeling. "It cannot be so."

Two dealers are making a house call to a 17th century Connecticut home. They have been there before but never allowed upstairs. After many years they head up to the second floor and attic. In the latter they find 300 years of objects. One of them discovers and uncovers a remarkable Queen Anne/ William and Mary armchair, all original including the leather (cracked), with ramshorn arms. They are speechless. The piece is breathtaking. It is amazing that it has survived, and it is the best of the best with 300 years of family history as provenance. I believe a Buddhist might say that it the chair decided to reenter the world after all this time.

Long standing collectors were in awe of an 18th century Pennsylvania schrank (large wardrobe or cupboard) that far exceeded their criteria for possession: The decoration spoke more loudly than the piece itself. They were overwhelmed by the nearly pristine original painted surface, its massive size, original bun feet and rat tail hinges. The schrank, the centerpiece of the couple's collection, remained in the dining room of their 19th century farmhouse for more than 20 years. As one of the finest extant and intact examples of 18th century Pennsylvania furniture, the schrank was donated to Winterthur Museum where it evokes reverence to this day.

Why is awe so important to collectors and dealers? Because they, like everyone else, have a need to be reminded from time to time of their place in the universe, their insignificance, and of mysteries that can never be explained. Collecting provides such experiences.

Dealers hope to educate collectors, to lead them to appreciate certain genres and to share the dealers' reverence for a marvelous piece. Reading once again Fruend's *Objects of Desire* (*The Lives of Antiques and Those Who Pursue Them*), I took away the same feeling of awe for the robin's egg blue Queen Anne blanket chest—plain to the point of never even having brasses—that the author feels for it. Its simple lines approach perfection, and its condition lacks any signs of material culture. It has stood in someone's bedroom or living room for 270 years. To the author and anyone who agrees with him, all of this is simply awe-inspiring.

I once asked a dealer friend why another dealer, whom I shall leave nameless, was so successful. I was told it was, in part, because he had a wonderful eye and a deep knowledge of American antiques. He could describe why a certain chair or painting was so very special when others might simply see one antique out of many. In thinking back to this conversation, I believe now that he holds certain antiques in reverence and is successful in educating collectors why these pieces do or should inspire awe.

I hypothesize that awe is a major reason why many collectors cherish silver crafted by Paul Revere. There were better silversmiths I am told, but none who are such an integral part of the story and myths of the American revolution. He is immortalized in Longfellow's poem of his midnight ride of 1775. To hold a piece of silver he crafted, the "man" who helped the American revolution succeed, is indeed awe-inspiring. Keltner in his book Awe, calls this a WHOA! moment, an apt description indeed, (though when used in conjunction with Paul Revere verging on a pun).

Finding awe in their collecting may have a profound effect on collectors of American antiques. For awe expands collectors' perspectives, encouraging them to revel in the feelings of joy of transcendence of these experiences. They may appreciate their lives more and take less for granted. Being in the presence of awe-inspiring antiques may encourage collectors' curiosity and search for knowledge. They may be inspired and think of their collection and hobby in new and different ways. We are back to where we began with Einstein's observation.

Briefly stated, experiencing awe enriches collectors' lives as they feel alive be in wonderment and their WHOA!

moments. There is something awe inspiring in a Nobel prize winner in physics (but not for his theory of relativity) and one of the greatest scientists to ever live who looked at the world with reverence and wonder. Even more unexpected and perhaps awe inspiring is that he is a role model for us all in attending to the mysteries of existence and our world, even the universe of American antiques. Collect with your eyes and heart open.

CHAPTER 8

Failure and Losing Out

Every collector loses out at some point; it does not matter if he collects million-dollar paintings or furniture, or $300 painted boxes. Collectors do not always get what they want, nor does anyone in real life. I certainly did not get the painting I coveted (cited as an example of resilience in Chapter 5). Collectors can bemoan how unfair that is, but life seems to work that way.

Given that losing out, failure, is an integral part of the collectors' world, how can they weather the storm? How do they deal with the feelings and knowledge that failing causes? My thesis: Collectors need to resign themselves to failing. They need to find a strategy that works for them, for accepting it will happen. They need to keep their objectivity. And for goodness' sake, keep their sense of fun and joy (few things are so rare and so precious that they cannot do without).

I think the collector's hunt going awry is as much the consequence of sheer luck's nasty side as it is collectors' behaviors. Both have their roles and play their parts well.

Since striking out is unavoidable, it would be silly to tell a collector to avoid failure. Simple resignation is surrender, of course. Collecting makes demands on us, and one the most difficult to accommodate is the sheer, oblivious testiness of a world that will not concede to our desires. Once we know that, we can live with failure; we can persevere through challenges and learn them. For in collecting Alfred, Lord Tennyson (the most famous Victorian era poet) hit the nail on the head writing: "It is "better to have loved and lost than never to have loved at all." In our world, of course, the beloved object may be a rare silver 18th century sugar bowl rather than someone we call "Sugar." And we take our lumps.

Why do collectors lose out? Sometimes they fail because other collectors have deeper pockets. Sometime dumb luck intervenes. Other antiques sell in minutes because of their quality, rarity, or the eccentricity of a particular buyer. Pieces are often bought out of the back of trucks and vans at shows or markets before even reaching the retail floor.

Serendipity can be a cruel mistress, too, when she does not favor a collector. Yes, life can be unfair, as any collector knows being one of the first fifty folks in line at a show does not guarantee the piece will be hers.

When assessing losing out, the smart collector looks first and deepest at her own behaviors. "Did I do everything I could to maximize the chance the table would be mine?" If the answer is "yes" the collector may feel dismayed or frustrated but can move forward knowing she was not the cause of the loss. I encourage bold, unflinching and honest self-assessment. No excuses. Finally, do not punish yourself if things do not work out; learn from them. If a collector has done all she can—due diligence for example—she can hope that things even out in the long run, that the next piece, or the one after that shall be hers. We call that hope.

To maximize hope, collectors need to work vigorously to maximize the chances of prevailing. (Yes, being near the front of show lines does have an effect, even it if is not always perfectly successful.) Try not to be too envious of a collector who has a run of success in building his collection.

He is probably working very hard at it and still has missed opportunities and made mistakes of which you are unaware.

The highchair is a piece I felt strongly about. I did not want to miss out on it. A collector needs to be vigorous and active over time to increase the chances of success, and vigorously active I nearly failed to be in this instance. I loved the highchair's image in color photographs. It arrived as part of an email from dealers doing the Antiques in Manchester Collector's Fair. I initially paid it little attention because I assumed we could not afford it. Clayton Pennington in his April 2024 editorial in *Maine Antique Digest* urged collectors to "buy the dip," get things while the getting's good, while the market has adjusted to lower prices. None the less I did not believe the "dip" applied to this wonderful antique. Once again, an error on my part.

I bring Karen Herbert Disaia, the promoter of the Collector's Fair, flowers each year to thank her for allowing me space in a booth at the show when my first book on collecting was newly published (*Come Collect with Me*). It was generous of her, and I appreciate her doing so to this day. Having completed my mission in 2024 I was schmoozing with two of the show's workers at the entrance the afternoon before the show opened. Lo and behold the dealers offering the highchair walked in. I called out to her and queried what she was asking for the piece. To my great surprise it was eminently affordable. I said so. After all, the condition was wonderful, the turning superb, its small size delightful, the upper stretcher a treat with centuries of wear. When I was done talking, she told me she might have to revise her pricing structure. I laughed.

I asked for the chair's dimensions, specifically its width and depth. One of the workers was glad to accompany me so I could measure it, but I told her it was a cardinal sin for a collector to be in a show before it opened. It gave me an unfair advantage as I would know of other offerings as booths were set up. If word got out, I expected to be the recipient of some fellow collectors' ire. So, she went and measured it. I stayed put.

The next morning, I arrived very early so I would be near the front of the line and when the show opened made a beeline for the chair. It was even better in person than in the photo and soon sported a red dot that means sold. This was one hunt that I was determined would not go amiss.

But collectors must beware of what is known as the "gambler's fallacy." Collectors should not assume that bad luck will necessarily be followed by good luck. That losing out now will mean they succeed later. Keep in mind that flipping a coin three times and having it come up heads does not mean the next flip is likely to be tails; the odds are still 50-50.

A natural part of failure to bring home a wonderful addition to one's collection is to look beyond oneself. There is a temptation to behave the way a seven-year-old does when asked, "Who broke the living room lamp?" pointing to his brother or sister (or the dog or cat) and proclaiming, "It wasn't me, he did it." Indulging in the so-called "blame game" —even if called for (I put the piece at the show on hold, but the dealer sold it out from under me. Or, The auction house misrepresented the piece, so how was I to know?)— may soothe a collectors wounded ego, avoid responsibility, or lessen disappointment but in the long run is not terribly educational or productive. Suppose you made a basic mistake. After putting a piece on hold, you failed to return to the dealer's booth promptly or even ignored it for a time, leaving the vendor to wonder whether the offer was serious, or you had left the show. Being a businessman, he sells the chair, table, or painting to another collector on the bird-in-the-hand principle. Keen as you might, excuse as you can. The truth is, it was your blunder.

The chest of drawers pictured has positive characteristics. Tiger maple is very desirable, the piece's 36-inch width improves how it looks to the eye, its height is excellent, the replacement brasses look original, and the side cutouts are superb. (You will have to trust me about the cutouts.) But the top is a replacement. It probably took someone as long to pick out the tiger maple for the top and fashion it as it did the original craftsman to make the entire chest. The chest was purchased from dealers we had known for years and done business with before. They had not given it a thorough once over and did not know the top was not right. It was only when we had our collection appraised years ago that we learned of the chest's newer addition.

In essence, the top is too good—the tiger maple superb with its graining and the thumb nail molding. It is not difficult to learn the top is not original to the piece if one removes the top drawer, flashlight in hand, and gives a thorough look at it. That is something the dealers and we did not do. The error is ours. The question of course is whether we would have purchased the piece if we had known of the newer top. The price might have been a bit lower, but the chest would have looked the same. I have never truly answered that question. Over the years we have not upgraded it. So perhaps the answer lies in our subsequent (to purchase) behavior. Yet the mistake niggles me to this day.

I learned, and this took place early in my collecting life, to look closely at pieces, that dealers expect a collector to do so, that it is a necessity, that it is part of being a collector.

The fact we still have the chest and enjoy it suggests

a more important reality. Some errors in collecting are more grievous than others. Aside from the top, the chest is a good one. The chest illustrates the observation that collectors lie on a purist continuum. Sandy and I typically like furniture that is original or has only acceptable replacements and modifications (the replacement brasses on the tiger maple chest are acceptable). But a replacement top is certainly not "acceptable" to many collectors. I conclude that as collectors in this case we are not purists. Lastly, relationships stamp their impression on collectors and their collections. The chest was purchased from the dealers who long ago educated us on collecting and high-country furniture, Bernice and Jim Miller. To upgrade the chest with a replacement has always felt like losing part of them. This fact leads to another important point: Collectors hang on or upgrade antiques in their collection for many reasons.

Collectors must hold themselves to a high standard, including admitting and learning from their own mistakes Yes, looking in a mirror can be hard psychological work. Pointing at yourself and saying, "I blew it" may not feel good. But introspection and making sense of what transpired can lead to fewer losses in the future, and better collecting behaviors. Passing the buck runs the real risk of perpetuating mistakes and raising the likelihood of future failures.

Auctions can be exciting because a collector never knows what will happen. Buying a piece amidst auction fever and beyond the price limit a collector set for himself is not uncommon. That set of chairs the bidder won may have been a bargain simply because the collector he was competing with was occupied with a phone call, fatigued from a problem at work, or distracted by a crisis at home. If a collector overpaid, however, or she was unsuccessful, she needs to realize it is all part of the collecting game. But she would be wise to look at why she overspent or missed out.

I recently had such an experience. After looking for a Windsor bench for some years, my wife and I had given up finding one. In writing this chapter it struck me that I had not let several dealers who were likely to come across such a bench know that I was seeking one. Why I failed to do so until recently mystifies me, since I have made inquiries in the past for other pieces I was seeking. All I could do was shake my head at myself and get in touch with dealers, knowing that now I was better positioned to find such a bench in the future if one exists in our price-point. If I fail to find such a bench now, I am aware I have done all I can.

Do not lose sight of the fact that not all losses, not all failures as a collector are created equal. Overpaying greatly for an object because a collector is unaware of the market is avoidable and signals a fundamental failure of conscientiousness, research, and discipline That was a piece a collector wanted to miss out on. As is a piece up for auction that a collector believes, as the auction house claims is 18th or early 19th century only to learn it was a reproduction after purchasing it. A smart collector would ask someone knowledgeable to look at it during preview, avoiding a major "oops." Errors like that can be costly, not to mention ego deflating.

Collectors had best get used to looking in the mirror because the types and number of mistakes they can make are many and varied. Learn from one experience and avoid it in the future? All well and good until another scenario arises and another lapse in judgment occurs.

One way to adjust to missing out is to keep the following in mind: "Try again. Fail again. Fail better" (Samuel Beckett - Irish novelist, playwright, short story writer, theatre director, and poet). Fail better is the idea that a collector can choose the relationship he has with failure. He can be devasted by it and fearful, or he can learn from it. If a collector wants certainty, he should rapidly walk away from collecting as a hobby.

By adopting the "fail better" maxim, and it may take time, collectors learn not to be threatened by failure. It happens to everyone. Keep in mind that if you bat .300 in baseball you have a good chance to end up in Cooperstown's Baseball Hall of Fame. At the same time, that legendary batter will have made an out seven times for every ten at bat. Sandy and I enjoy the tiger maple chest and have made peace with our mistake. We failed better.

Not to belabor the point but collectors also come to realize that there is nothing wrong with feeling badly if they miss out or screw up. Yeah, it does not feel good, but it is not supposed to (see Chapters 5 on Resilience and 10 on Grief.) The feeling is a natural outcome of loss. It often slows people down, is a stimulus for introspection and realization, sometimes to insight, and for collectors the reality that they must soldier on. Approaching a collecting disaster analytically by parsing what took place and whether this is becoming a pattern may serve a collector well.

Collectors best be aware of compensating for their failures by compounding them. A collector who has lost out on a wonderful painting is doing herself and her collection no favors if she turns around and buys a so-so one. Equally problematic she could overbid or overpay on the next one that becomes available, even though it is not quite as good. It seems part of our nature to be seen as winners, to be viewed (by ourselves and others) as succeeding. Collectors should stick with their connoisseurship, passion and diligence. But to be honest, sometimes doing so is difficult.

Have I made collecting mistakes besides not alerting certain dealers to my quest for a Windsor bench? Yes. As you have read, the nice tiger maple chest of drawers in one bedroom has a replaced top. Then there was the hooked rug with a house, two animals, trees, and more. I waited too long at a show to purchase it. I still shake my head, "Why didn't I at least put it on hold?" That mistake also is one I have not repeated. Not purchasing this textile mystifies me to this day. I have never seen another one and I liked it! The lipstick red small box pictured in Chapter 22 is still another. And I more recently purchased some nice shaker brushes we really have no place to display. Oops.

Perhaps some losses (mistakes) are inexplicable? I take solace from that thought (but still learned from my mistake). Ask someone who specializes in some narrow, well-researched field of antiques—a (fill in the blank genre) for example—whether he has ever bought a piece that he thought was period and unrestored, that had every sign of being 18th century, that other collectors thought was the same, that was ... uh, what? That is what lessons look like. So, with grace, collectors persevere.

Bad luck and the personal tics, prejudices, blind spots, preferences, and lapses of individual collectors lead to missing out and screwing up, yet they are all part and parcel of the art of collecting. All collectors have scars and blemishes they have acquired over the years. A collector's star may not burn as brightly as he wishes sometimes. But that is true for everyone. Be self-aware.

I hope that your luck as a collector is good over time and that you continue to improve your collecting acumen. And when things do not go your way, hang in there. Success is just around the corner until you again "fail better."

CHAPTER 9

Gratitude

It is time to spend a moment or two being thankful and appreciative for what collecting American antiques (or any genres) adds to collectors' lives. It is a good endeavor, and the fact that it is so should not be taken for granted. How lucky these collectors are to have American antiques as one of their day-to-day activities.

Generally speaking, we are thankful when something good happens to us. Typically, we experience gratitude because we are aware that someone is responsible for the act of goodness or kindness—a friend, a stranger, an impersonal source, or even the divine.

The experience of gratitude varies person to person, collector to collector. As a trait it seems that some people experience gratitude more frequently than others. The feeling of gratitude as a mood varies over time and is hard to hold onto. Gratitude is a positive emotion and can be experienced even when one is at a low ebb, when other aspects of one's life are not going well. It should be noted that gratitude does not come automatically or, to some people easily. It is human to think that all the good that comes to us is either due to our personal efforts or deserved. When we are thankful, we turn attention away from ourselves and toward others.

What then do collectors have to be thankful for? Who do they want to acknowledge? What follows is my list of those deserving of collector gratitude. Readers may have others to whom they are grateful that I have omitted. To whom should collectors offer their thanks? Let us begin our discussion with mentors.

Early Mentors

Collectors need to give thanks to their early mentors who held their hands, educated them, showered them with patience and information, and opened the door to what for many has been a long-lived endeavor. Depending on the age of the collector, many of these mentors are deceased. We should not forget them. They can be remembered by mentioning their names to others, by emulating them as seasoned collectors and dealers take their places and mentor the next generation in the American antique universe, and by what we collect. Our earliest mentors Bernice and Jim Miller taught Sandy and me about high-country American antiques which formed and continue to make up the heart of our collection. Our collection to this day reflects their values that became our own—original surfaces, wooden works clocks, and looking for the best we could afford in different genres.

My wife and I became friends with our early mentors, something not unusual as I talk with others who had the same experience. Thus, our lives were not only enriched by conversations about American antiques and the goings on in the marketplace, but by time spent talking about children, classic cars, and the like.

Mentors Along the Way and in the Present

As collectors branch out, work with a variety of dealers and explore new genres, even if they have been collecting for some time, new mentors enter their collecting world. Certainly, many of these mentors make a living from what they sell to us, if dealers, but others are fellow collectors. The truth is that learning about Americana never ceases despite the years spent collecting. In my case, only late in the game did I become interested in redware with writing on it, Hudson valley paintings, and redware banks. These relatively recent interests opened the door to meeting and talking with mentors I would not have had otherwise.

I have been collecting redware banks for about four years. Those pictured represent the best forms I could find to date. I erred on one I do not own. I should have bid higher at an auction. At the time I was somewhat lazy about the marketplace. Better knowledge of what superb examples were selling for would have led to a higher bid by me. These banks have no opening in the bottom to remove the coins inserted in them. Often the slot has been widened so that it is easier to shake out the saved half-cents and cents.

Collecting these banks has put me in touch with several dealers and auction houses that were new to me, and I find it refreshing to talk with them. While *caveat emptor* is my collector responsibility, all have been helpful. I continue to look for more such banks, and I shall persevere.

Upgrading a collection also leads to new mentors. As dollars become available and collectors upgrade their collections, they may find themselves working with new (to them) dealers, in need of advice on pieces up for auction, and learning to discriminate between different examples of "better" or "best." "Each of us has cause to think with deep gratitude of those who have lighted the flame within us." (Albert Schweitzer)

Show Promoters

It was the obituary and remembrances of Sanford (Sandy) Smith in early summer 2024, show promoter extraordinaire (art shows, book fairs, the Modernism show, the first all-American show) that made me realize how important these folks are to collectors and the American antiques world. Promoters make the wonderful shows happen that collectors might take for granted. They, as was the case with Sandy Smith, open the eyes of collectors to new genres and design. More than one dealer in their memories and praise of him after his death said he put folk-art and Americana "on the map."

Shows only get good dealers if promoters treat them right. Promoters fight for wonderful venues and then keeping them. A good promoter is concerned about his dealers doing well financially. They are equally adept at wiring, easy loading and unloading for dealers, air conditioning and other mundane aspects that are the core of a first-rate antique show.

And they never lose sight of the collectors who will be reaching for their wallets. Good food, nearby parking, and a fine array of offerings are just a few of the ways a show promoter remembers these collectors.

Fellow Collectors

A sense of community and camaraderie in the American antique world cannot be complete without the relationships that collectors form with others. These collectors ask about one's health or steer the way to a booth that has just the antique a collector said she was looking for in line before a show opened. Based on past experiences they often recommend a dealer a fellow collector might want to explore and work with. My experience is that collectors, while they sometimes compete for the same piece, depend on each other in a wide variety of ways.

I have found fellow collectors to be supportive and friendly as they describe their collections, regale others with stories (as I do), and help each other out. Standing in line for three hours or more gives collectors lots of time to schmooze. A few years ago, I was talking with a husband and wife, whose names I have forgotten, probably in their early 60s. I learned they had remodeled their kitchen in the preceding year and had deliberately left a spot for a small fowl weathervane. While not experts on vanes they had done some reading in the prior months and hoped to fill that spot so their kitchen would be complete. But they were at a loss of which dealers to trust and work with. I named two or three to help them out. The doors opened some time after that conversation and in we went. The aisles were crowded as the 500 or more collectors in line filled the venue. The couple went their way, and I went mine.

After only a few minutes, I entered the booth of a dealer I had bought weathervanes from in the past whom I had recommended to them. He is known for "honest" vanes. And there, staring me in the eye, was a small weathervane of a rooster (if I remember right). It had original surface and crowed to me. Out I went, battling the crowds until I literally ran into the woman, her husband nowhere to be found. Taking her by the hand I led (perhaps dragged is more accurate as time was of the essence) her to the dealer's booth. Her husband somehow had spotted us and miraculously appeared. I told them the dealer was to be trusted in my opinion, and they ought to purchase the vane on the spot. After the dealer described the piece to them and their education complete (at least for the moment) they did just that. And I am sure they would do the same for me.

Dealers

The last chapter in *The Collector's World* (2021) is a paean for American antique dealers. I felt they were under-appreciated and deserving of plaudits—"hard working entrepreneurs who live by their wits, knowledge, dedication, and sheer stubbornness." Where would collectors be without them? They are deserving of collectors' applause. Their knowledge is born on the road of experience, yet they share it with collectors gratis. Their love for history is contagious. Working with collectors they strive to improve their connoisseurship. More recently, dealers have had to do more work for less profit.

Dealers are relevant and deserving of collectors' respect and acknowledgement. After all, they must deal with "us" (collectors) daily. They are well versed in collectors' foibles. They ply their trade in a capitalistic market, having mastered the art of buying and selling and making a living. Dealers are collectors' Sacagawea, their guides just as she assisted the Lewis and Clark expedition.

The Periodical and Book World

Where would collectors of American antiques be without the publications on which they depend so much? *Maine Antique Digest, Antiques and the Arts Weekly (The Bee), The Magazine Antiques*, other periodicals, and a host of books replete with history and heritage. The Chipstone Foundation, located near Milwaukee, supports the publication of the best of research on an annual basis. Collectors have a wealth of researchers to reach out to at museums to learn more about antiques in their collections.

These tomes and weekly, monthly or bi-monthly publications teach collectors, affirm their connections to the past through the genres they collect and their appreciation for the material culture these pieces bring with them. They keep collectors up to date on the market, upcoming auctions, shows, and other events, museum offerings and the like. The amount of work seems endless and detailed. I do not know how the editors, reporters, contributors, and other staff do the sterling job that they do. Remembering those who have passed on, offering opinion and a town square for readers to weigh in, in-depth research about craftsmen as several examples.

Each publication in its own way affirms the connoisseurship and visual appeal of collecting American antiques, attesting to the beauty and aesthetics collectors value so much and that play such a significant role in their collecting. They are a venue for the passion collectors feel and allow them to share it with others. They also support the preservation and conservation of American antiques and a way of life from the 17th century and beyond. I believe I am not overstating their value when I praise the periodical and book world. It brings personal fulfillment and enjoyment to collectors.

Each of us has cause to thank with deep gratitude those who have lighted the flame within us. As a collector of American antiques, I offer gratitude for the history, craftsmanship, beauty, community, preservation efforts, and personal fulfillment that collecting provides. These elements enrich collectors' passions and deepen their connection to the objects they collect.

Even if what we collect is considered merely "stuff" by some others, and they are wrong my friends, they are wrong, our antiques provide an avenue to a wonderful world larger than ourselves. Kindness seems to be the coin of the realm in the American antique universe. We should not take each other for granted. You may want to let some of these people in your collecting life know how appreciative you are. Such gratitude may have a big impact.

These then are the people I am grateful for and wanted to acknowledge. Collectors have much to be thankful for when they look at their world. When younger and a newer collector I took others more for granted than I do now. Positive relationships and a sense of community should be cherished, and my appreciation has grown over the years. I am thankful for the positive influence they have all had on my collecting life.

CHAPTER 10
Grief

Collecting is a microcosm of life, oftentimes writ large. It follows then that the universe of Americana must contain loss and the response to it, grief. Writers set a stage and place their actors upon it, endowing them with thoughts, feelings, and actions appropriate to an author's intentions and goals. My stage here acknowledges grief as part and parcel of the collectors' lot.

We tend to think of grief as a response to the death or loss of a living creature (human or beloved pet for example) we love, esteem, or respect—spouses, children, dear friends, people influential in our lives in one way or another. Those who have collected Americana for any length of time have made friends with fellow collectors, dealers, auction house folks, and others. When one of them passes on grief knocks at these collectors' doors. Oftentimes such grief feels as if one has lost a family member, which in its own way is true.

At the same time, we also can grieve the loss of a job or physical limitations due to illness or aging. And we can grieve the loss of things. While the emotional response to such loss is well known to many people, anyone who has experienced grief knows it has physical, behavioral, and spiritual manifestations—sorrow, heartache, pain, loss of appetite, disturbance of sleep, the unfairness that life goes on for most others. Despite the yearning for an acknowledged pathway of grief (Am I grieving appropriately? Is what I am experiencing part of grief?) there is no one way or certain way to grieve. I think of the popular five stages of grief, a theory first introduced by Elisabeth Kübler-Ross in her 1969 book *On Death and Dying* (denial, anger, bargaining, depression, acceptance) that has no research support.

Grief is more powerful (and less common) than sadness. Yes, we may be sad if we lose in an auction, or a dealer has sold a piece we really loved. But that is not grief.

It is time to turn to collectors' grief over lost objects. We form attachments with so many different people and things in our lives that it is not surprising that the loss of material objects, in our specific case, pieces of Americana, would trigger a grief response if the situation elicits one. If someone close to us dies and their collection dispersed or is no longer available to us, we may grieve the loss of such pieces. These antiques, as one dealer pointed out to me, had or (now have) a power that exceeds the aesthetic. They were part of the people we miss so and just as he or she was taken away so are these powerful remembrances of them. Isn't that why when a beloved dealer dies, collectors often seek out a piece at auction or for sale that once was his? The antique (as a transitional object) helps us keep alive the dealer and allows us to grieve his passing.

Well known to collectors is the fact that they remember the antiques that "got away" much more clearly than almost any in their present collections. Such crystalized memories are a form of grief and may be accompanied by wistfulness, anger (at themselves, at the world at large, at the antique gods, at their poor luck), a subdued mood, and if they are honest some interesting observations into their collectors' psyche. "Oh how I loved it so," they may say. "I can still see it as clear as the day I first encountered it." "If it came back on the market there is no price that I would not pay to be reunited with it." Grief is an intense reaction to failure and losing out and tells the collector to pay attention to what transpired.

Another way to lose a treasured object is through simple breakage. It falls of a shelf; a collector is showing it to a peer and drops it. I think of a simple homespun blanket at home sitting in a basket I had neglected for far too long. When I looked at it a moth hole or two mocked me. I was heartsick and grieved the loss of a perfectly formed textile, now ruined and kicked myself for my neglect as well.

No one can collect without being disappointed time and time again. Disappointment is like a "small death," a "tolerable loss," of something hoped for even if to others the matter seems trivial. "You are going through that(!) because you did not get an old painted box?" a friend might say. "Heck yes," the collector replies. "It would have been the *piece de resistance* of my collection. It encompassed years of collecting and even more yearnings. I mourn its loss." What has happened is that losing out, for whatever reason on that painted box has undermined this collector's sense of self; it has damaged his identity. Such sabotage, subversion and threats to our well-being as a collector can easily precipitate grief. The collector is grieving as much for himself as he is for the lost love (painted box).

In other cases, vandalism or outright theft, or a catastrophe (home fire, hurricane, tornado) may lead to the loss of beloved antiques. The grief at times like this is palatable. What has been lost, of course, is more than the objects themselves. The objects, now gone forever, can no longer be touched. It is only photographs of them that elicit memories, that used to be warm and sustaining, with stories accompanying them, now bitter and empty. It is difficult to come to terms with the vicissitudes of life sometimes, the unfairness and capriciousness of mother nature, for example. Grief is a natural response to such loss.

Grief is one of the more complicated processes we encounter in our lives. We may grieve for decades over some losses. The loss of a child is so unimaginable that the English language lacks a word to label a parent who has had a child die. Aeschylus, an ancient Greek tragedian (often considered the father of tragedy) highlighted grief's complex nature when he wrote, "There is no pain so great as the memory of joy in present grief." For what is grief but painful love. We strive to remember the best of those we grieve for including the "memory of joy" and collectors are no exception.

A dropleaf kitchen table, circa 1860, some sort of hard-wood, perhaps maple. The top needs work. The table is battered. It presents much better in the photograph than it truly is. It has been used in our household for almost 55 years. It does not fit with our collection. Its era, finish, and style place it in jarring contrast to other antiques we own. Yet it remains. My wife insists. The table is magical, almost a talisman in how it calls forth memories. We pulled highchairs up to it when we fed our two boys. We broke bread with dear friends for hours at this table—laughing, reminiscing, telling stories. The friends are gone now, our sons long out of the home. To sell the table would invoke grief. Grief not just for those memories but for ourselves. "Where has the time gone?" "How is it we are old now?" "What has happened in and to our lives?" So, the table sits where it has always sat, the grief avoided for the moment, but in the background, almost on the edges of our awareness, waiting. To keep the table is to forestall (some of) the grief we would feel.

In this example, my wife is sensitive to and has experienced what is known as anticipatory grief. Typically, such grief occurs before someone has died, someone for example with a devastating disease, in hospice perhaps. Most people who have lived a long life have experienced such grief. My wife has grieved the table's loss even though it is still with us. She knows some of what she will experience if it were to be replaced. Those feelings have cemented her resolve to keep it (and I can only agree with her about her feelings and decision).

As another dealer reminded me, we also can grieve the loss of knowledge. A "go-to" person who has forgotten more than most people know dies. And with him the Americana community loses some of what he had learned and taught in his lifetime. I think of Wayne Pratt and Cahoon paintings and Nantucket baskets, Bradley and his Chester County knowledge Mel Wolf, the doyen of American pewter. Still alive is Jim Kilvington—Delaware idiosyncrasies, John Keith Russell—Shaker, Jeffrey Tillou—Chambers' Hudson Valley paintings, and I am only scratching the surface. When individuals such as these and far more unmentioned leave the Americana universe their understanding and learning, built up over a lifetime, largely disappears. One can only hope for apprentices and able students to replace them.

But a need to put things in perspective is called for. Collectors need to be careful about over-reactions and "false" reactions. A word of caution—it is possible to attach too much significance to most transitory things. Loss is part of life, and the sense of loss some of the time is hardly unhealthy or symptomatic of anything but taking oneself and one's possessions far too seriously

The child wailing because his blankie is in the wash has the same dire sense of loss that the collector whose Picasso is lost in a fire does. The difference in value is terrific, but does that make the emotion any less? In fact, assuming the art-owner is mature, there ought to be three understandings: (1) what we collect is mutable and may have survived this long by luck, (2) the loss is not only to oneself but, more importantly, to our sense of history, place and meaning, and (3) objects can be as real in memory as they are on the shelf in the keeping room or sitting in our living room (and memory ought to be cultivated as an essential element of the collecting art).

In all its manifestations "grief is the price we pay for love" (Queen Elizabeth II). Those in the American antique world love each other, the objects that awe them, the material culture that speaks to decades and centuries, to preserving the history of our nation. If on occasion, grief is the price we must pay for that love, pay it we shall.

CHAPTER 11

Joy and Contentment

Let us move from failure, losing out and grief to feelings that make collecting so pleasurable. I start with joy, for it sustains collectors. If collectors have not experienced joy at seeing or purchasing certain pieces, they have a wonderful experience to look forward to.

Joy is described as a brief feeling of exuberance, a minor uplift that makes elation seem like plain vanilla. A feeling of jubilation, triumph, exultation. A metaphoric thumping of one's heart. The gods have been defeated; one stands on top of the mountain. I am immortal. A feeling that opens a person up to the world, reaching out to others, that a collector wants to share.

I have written about what rewards the collector—aesthetic appreciation, feelings of happiness or fulfillment (the meaning collecting provides), perhaps the intellectual realm of scholarship or research that illuminates. Much more transitory but not to be overlooked is the feeling of joy.

A collector walks a show. It is I. I have been looking for a Hudson Valley painting by Thomas Chambers (pictured in Chapter 7 and on the book's cover). And there one is, and it is gorgeous, as good a piece of folk-art as I could have dreamed of. Being near the front of the show line I have the opportunity make an offer. The dealer's price is fair; it is mine. And symbolically I want to do a dance in the dealer's booth, emulating NFL or Premier League soccer players who have scored a touchdown or goal. The burst of energy makes me smile, brings warmth to my heart. Oh, the joys of collecting.

As a powerful, positive emotion, it is no wonder that joy reinforces and maintains collectors. Like sunshine that brings warmth and light to us, joy also brings light and warmth to collectors' lives. It brightens them.

The feeling is much briefer than feelings of contentment. I will feel contented on the long trip home as I reflect on my good fortune, a feeling of peace and gratitude for what collecting adds to my life. I will be able, and have been able, to look at and appreciate the painting daily. But the intense memory of "goal accomplished" will resonate, even if the feeling itself has dissipated.

For it is discontentment with a collector's pieces that motivate him to continue the hunt. And if the hunt, over time, is successful, the collector can bask in contentment as he puts his feet up long after a show has ended or a visit to a dealer's shop has concluded.

Contentment seems to have more sources than joy and is more readily available. Collectors can feel contented looking at their collections. They may feel contented reading this publication or others and comparing their collections to antiques displayed at shows, auction houses or in dealers' advertisements. Feelings of contentment may arise when they talk with other collectors. Not as intense as joy, contentment has its own power and importance. Contentment is the product of reflection; joy is the result of the moment.

Some people describe feelings of joy as a precious gift that they want to hold onto but cannot. While not easily forgotten joy is a delight. Both joy and contentment are to valued and cherished. "Collecting is good, it is worthwhile, it is an endeavor I want to continue" the collector tells himself. Joy has been described as a warm embrace; the collector feels safe, life's challenges and struggles put aside for the moment.

A collector does not have to purchase a desired antique to experience joy. Simply being in the presence of a wonderful piece can elicit the feeling. Visits to museums or auction house previews, or simply being stopped in one's tracks at a show with feelings of "wow" can give rise to joy. Feelings of continuing learning, developing one's connoisseurship, and time with friends in the Americana community maintain and enhance a collector's contentment. Simply helping fellow collectors, be they new or experienced can add to contentment—"You were looking for a piece of redware and the dealer in booth number 12 has a good example," or "Let's take a look at that box you are considering and decide if the paint is original" are examples I have personally experienced.

Yet when collectors look deeper and examine their own experiences, I believe they will find that only a few pieces in their collection brought joy when first seen and then purchased. The reason is because joy is not easily or commonly achieved. The positive events that elicit joy are often rare and unpredictable, making joy even more precious because of its fleeting nature and the impossibility of sustaining it.

I walked through my home looking at pieces of Americana in my wife's and my collection. As is true of most collectors I can remember where and when almost each was purchased. Our home is full, my wife's dictum echoes: Nothing comes into the house unless something goes out (except jewelry). She is a wise woman. Why does joy so seldom appear? Let me reverse the question: What caused joy in the few pieces that did or do so in our home?

Three paintings of the many that grace the walls (and sit on the floor) did so. One is of a schooner I wrote about and it (and pictured) in *Come Collect with Me*. It captures a spirit and way of life now gone. I have always loved the sea despite growing up in the heartland, reading *Horatio Hornblower*, *Master and Commander*, *Moby Dick*, *Captain Blood* and others. Once I purchased the schooner painting, I read several books about schooners and their role in our country in the transportation of goods. I concluded I was "primed" to have the painting bring me joy. It captured my long-standing fantasy of a life at sea.

The second painting is the Thomas Chambers' Hudson Valley depiction of the *View from West Point* referred to above (and pictured in Chapter 7). It took my breath away. I have always loved the water (looking at it, not being in it). Growing up in Chicago Lake Michigan was my ocean. There is something about Chambers' work that pulls together the various elements depicted in a beautiful way. Again, it was as if I had waited my entire life for this painting. It fits my dreams and needs.

The third is pictured here. Victor DeGrailly was a better trained and a more formal artist than Chambers. The scene is the same as in Chambers' painting, but this is not a piece of folk-art. I did not know of DeGrailly's work before seeing it pictured on a dealer's website of inventory. Seeing it before it became ours made me smile. It is a wonderful depiction of the Hudson from West Point. There is something peaceful and beautiful about the scene that DeGrailly captured. There is something joyful that is difficult to convey about having both Chambers' and DeGrailly's paintings of the same scene.

In talking with several collectors, they shared the experience that an antique or collectible that tied them to past loves or likes seemed to elicit joy. Postcards for one, original Nancy Drew books for another, Star Wars items for a third, Connecticut Valley pieces for a fourth that remind him of the towns and hamlets he spent time in decades ago. Then there is an antique silver teapot I discuss as a "find" in Chapter 20 where it is pictured as well.

Lastly, is a piece of high-country furniture: a dropfront desk pictured on the cover of *Come Collect with Me*. I think it is its "perfection" and evidence of material culture that brought such a smile to my face when I first saw it. "You mean I can own this?" "I can live with this?" "This can be mine"? As I listen to those statements, they sound kind of crass to me. But this desk was better than I had ever dreamed of adding to our collection. It fit in its own way, a preconceived notion I had of what the desk of my dreams would look like gracing our living room. I am unclear how that dream came about. How does any collector formulate an object of their dreams? And then have their dreams realized? Perhaps it is an object that meets and surpasses any sense of aesthetic appreciation the collector may have.

Joy and contentment are guiding beacons for collectors, maintaining an optimism about both collecting and their future endeavors. The feelings are unexpected gifts. The classical notion is that they arise out of behaving in ways that people define as good, in other words as being virtuous. According to this idea, joy appears when people act congruent with their more angelic side or when experiencing positive interactions with the world. Happy occasions often elicit joy—a wedding, birth of a child or grandchild. Often collectors' joy springs from the shadows, a surprise the collector best enjoy in the moment while he can. Understanding joy and contentment is almost philosophic in nature.

Music has its magnificent Ode to Joy, Wordsworth's "Surprised by Joy" The former is, like the joy I have experienced as a collector, a paean to uplift. The latter is a realization that amid pain (he started writing it as a remembrance of his two dead children) there arises a blinding moment of appreciation of something that was and is gone. Joy does not have a single note, a single dimension; it is complicated. My reveries of things and persons lost sometimes have that little edge of sunlight around them.

Collectors may not have thought about it, but Robert Lewis Stevenson struck to the heart of collecting when he said, "...Find out where joy resides, and give it a voice far beyond singing. For to miss the joy is to miss all." All any collector can say in response is "Amen."

CHAPTER 12

Love and Desire

Some enchanted evening, when you find your true love,
When you hear her call you across a crowded room,
Then fly to her side and make her your own,
Or all through your life you may dream all alone.
Once you have found her, never let her go,
Once you have found her, never let her go.

South Pacific, Richard Rodgers

Anyone who collects likes or loves the pieces he purchases, or in retrospect, at least most of them. At first perhaps, with a house to fill, liking or expediency for the collector takes precedence over love. But as connoisseurship and the collector's eye improves engaging in "the hunt" and leads to feelings of desire, of wanting, of loving. For some collectors, those labels may not truly capture what they feel when they fall in love with an antique. Lust may be a more accurate label for when pieces seduce them with a throaty "come hither." Many collectors find the alluring qualities of the antique they look at and touch almost dangerous, as love can be (at least to their pocketbook).

American antiques truly are *Objects of Desire* as Freund described them in his 1993 book. Love is indeed a motivational force and can lead to behaviors that to others appear irrational. Love involves a total preoccupation and focus on a person or object. People love and long for all sorts of things. It motivates them to offer millions for an automobile ($143 million is the record—a Mercedes Benz purchased in 2022) just as it underlies the stratospheric amounts paid for some items at auction when two collectors each decide he must own the piece. Prince Badr bin Abdullah Al Saud paid $450 million for the Salvator Mundi in 2017. It was painted by Leonardo da Vinci, or was it? For love can overcome rational thought and the boundaries of "normal" behavior.

Love is the stuff of novels, television shows, movies, poems, the theater, teenage and real life. Replace these scenes and themes with the voices of special antiques, and heroes and heroines with collectors, and the images remain valid and powerful. Yes, the pull of antiques, the ardent longing, the intense enthusiasm to possess, can be that strong, as many collectors know.

Love is a feverish desire for something or someone—a beautiful woman or handsome man, money, power, fame, antiques. Religions tend to draw a distinction between passion (acceptable) and lust (sinful). In early Christianity, a sin was considered a transgression against divine law. These transgressions were grouped into a set of vices—lust being one of the "seven deadly" sins. But as collectors know, when they find an antique of their dreams, what they feel if powerful enough may have a sinful tinge to it. Wherein lies the sin? Some suggest simply giving in is a wrong. The Puritanical suggest the accession to the thought is enough by itself.

Let us call that feeling extreme passion (and not lust) to remove the vestiges of sin.

It is somewhat ironical that after years of training one's eye, developing one's connoisseurship, developing an appreciation for the history of Americana and its objects, and what the material culture signifies, that a powerful feeling could be as or more important than all these combined in motivating and maintaining a collector's desires and spending. Head and heart (loins?). Shakespeare compares love with a form of madness, an observation with which most collectors are familiar and would probably agree. I certainly would. The collector finds powerful forces acting on him, and when a collector feels such power, he may become aware of his own powerlessness.

I offer a story of extreme love. I know a collector who long ago decided on the genre he would collect and has stuck to it to this day. When in college he purchased the first truly expensive piece for his collection at a cost of $21,000 (just under $31,000 in today's dollars). He was in college! It was an insane purchase, and he sold 20 to 30 pieces of nice stoneware, he does not remember exactly how many, to help finance the purchase as the cost was far more than he had dollars available. He still owns the piece and in retrospect he agrees that it was a "wildly irresponsible purchase. But I just couldn't say no," he told me. Even though the piece is worth less today, he has no regrets.

There is no doubt that love and desire are engines that keep the American antique world turning and churning. For "Lust's passion will be served; it demands, it militates, it tyrannizes" (Marquis de Sade). It certainly does as a motivator for the collectors many of us become. The anticipation of possessing a certain object is part and parcel of antiques being purchased every day and new record high prices for paintings, silver, and other genres. The antiques in question match collectors' templates for something in the world that must become theirs. They cannot live without them.

All of which got me thinking about American antiques I loved and what might have been had I purchased them. Even though hearty love is more than "I want that antique," or "I really want that antique," and is more like "I really, really, really want that antique," that does not mean the piece in question becomes part of a collector's collection. Sometimes all the robbing of Peter to pay Paul, the moving of money from one pot to another still will not cover its cost. Sometimes collectors must live with unrequited love. It is easy to for collectors to convince themselves that the pieces they let get away are the ones they loved the most. I am not sure that is true, but I can think of a baby blue blanket chest early in my collecting days when fiscal reality trumped my adoration.

In looking at my wife's and my collection I was struck by the pieces she or I had to own. We really, really, really wanted the Hoadley and Thomas wooden-works tall case clock with a great dial and painted case (pictured in *Come Collect with Me*). We were lucky; we could afford it, and we appreciate it to this day, as we do our tavern table in the living room and our New Hampshire, walnut, dropleaf Queen Ann dining room table (pictured in this chapter) and many other pieces. We are fortunate that we still find these antiques beautiful, for over time collectors may no longer love or even like objects they once yearned to possess. Love can be a fickle mistress.

The latter may seem a jarring comment but, alas, it is true. For I also was struck by the fact that my desire for these pieces is now but a dimming memory. For love over time cools, its heat ebbing into liking just as romantic love over time transforms itself. The best collectors can hope for is that a few pieces in their collection still kindle the flame of intense passion. Other pieces, once the objects of intense love, have probably become the objects of liking years later. Perhaps that is why collectors constantly upgrade their collection or begin collecting new genres.

Sandy and I are maximizers when it comes to dining room tables. The one pictured is our third (and last). The first was a country (not high-country) cherry table with round legs with turnings. Let us say circa 1860. We gave that table to one of our sons when we purchased a mahogany table with burl inlay on each side. Let us say circa 1820. It had tapering, Hepplewhite legs and was a looker but we were not satisfied. It went to our other son. A dealer we had kept in touch with knew of our love for high-country and our search for an even better table and sent us photos of the one we presently own. We were smitten. He offered to bring it to Wisconsin so we could see it in person. As it was uncovered in the van and made its egress, we knew we had to have it. Even before we brought it into the house, we had made up our minds. The feeling of desire was instantaneous.

The table looks especially lovely when the winter southern sun graces its surface. It is heavy with an understructure. One advantage of loving and desiring an American antique is if you are lucky enough to call it your own, you do not need to seek another (at least for a while).

And we may love in our hearts until confronted with fulfilling that endearment, and then change our minds. I once lusted after a wooden watch maker's sign in the shape of a clock face for some time, but when I encountered a fine example, I decided my ardor was misplaced and declined to purchase it. Oh, how we collectors drive ourselves (and dealers) mad sometimes!

Can a collector stop loving so deeply—perhaps? Identifying what pieces and situations trigger the feeling and sticking to whatever dollar amount he has set is a start. Some collectors prone to ardent love not only stop collecting but remove themselves entirely from the powerful stimuli that trigger that love in the first place—shows, auctions, dealers' shops and websites, (*The Bee*) *Antiques and the Arts Weekly*, or *Maine Antique Digest*.

By acknowledging what collecting means to him a collector can attempt to find alternative activities. Hard won wisdom may provide a solution. One collector I know well told me the following story.

I learned a long time ago that if it's meant to be, it will be. If not, it's not the end of the world. The older I get, the more I realize we are just caretakers of these things for a short period of time. If we don't get a particular item, it was meant for someone else, and I hope the item finds a good home. What I treasure most is the travel and the wonderful relationships I have built through the years with fellow collectors and dealers who have the same passion as I have. And that is all that really matters in the end.

When he saw the gameboard of his dreams, and he still speaks of it today in hushed tones, his perspective on collecting was stronger than mortgaging the farm to purchase it. I wish I had that discipline sometimes.

I continue to collect, and I find love is a closed loop—seeing antiques, loving one now and then, purchasing a loved item, love satisfied, love mellowing or fading over time (for many pieces), and then looking at antiques again. Lucky or cursed, I shall let you decide. What collectors love, what captures them, says a lot about them in the universe of antiques (and non-antiques) as well.

There you have it. Some argue that to be human is to desire what we do not have. It is said that passionate people achieve great things. "Each of us is born with a box of matches inside us but we can't strike them all by ourselves" says the novelist Laura Esquivel in her work, *Like Water for Chocolate*. But in our case, it is not the breath of someone else, the love from those in our lives that strikes the match on occasion, but the American antiques we collect. One could do worse, much worse as a collector. "For where there is love, there is life." (Mahatma Ghandi)

Chapter 13

Euphemisms

A euphemism is a mild or indirect word or phrase that substitutes for a well understood more direct description or adjective. You have a "questionable idea," not a bad idea. You did not throw up or vomit, you "lost your lunch." A more direct phrase or word may elicit more emotion and power, the former is softer and often meant not to hurt feelings. Why be blunt if one can avoid it? Why be clear if one can obfuscate?

Why indeed! More direct language often more accurately captures what one is describing but our society seems to be moving to more "civilized," some would say, speech. If someone from your organization's human resources tells you that you are being "let go" that has a softer tone than "you are fired." Pornography becomes "adult entertainment," the former sounds illegal and sordid, the latter not so much. Use of the word "prison" recalls Cagney in a black and white movie. "Correctional facility" seems to imply rehabilitation instead of retribution and "incarceration" does not even hint at crime. In a war civilian deaths might be termed "collateral damage." "Elected official" seems more civilized than politician, or heaven forbid, career politician.

Yes, tact and sensitivity have their place. But use of these polite, mild, or indirect words or phrases in place of an unpleasant one, softening or toning down the impact of the original word of phrase, has its problems. Euphemisms can obscure the true meaning or intention behind a statement (and lead a collector astray), resulting in confusion, miscommunication, or even deception. People can hide behind euphemisms and the true meaning of their statements.

I found myself pondering the Americana universe and the use of euphemisms therein. What phrases might collectors find that diplomatically address perceived flaws or negative qualities of antiques, perhaps hiding them in doing so? What phrases might collectors use to add "value" or to justify a recent purchased? I am sure I have not found them all but for entertainment I present the following.

As expected, is a term seen often in item descriptions. Yes, pieces from centuries past may have wear and tear. Many have been well used and that's a euphemism, too. The lack of such evidence of material culture may raise red flags. A chair without wear on the front stretcher for example. A dropfront desk with the lid pristine on the inside. But how much wear and tear is "expected," and how much begins to detract from the antique? "As expected," can be a euphemism for "crummy surface," or "lousy condition" In these cases, "you really can find better"—not a euphemism at all.

Conserved suggests a piece that is or was in a museum and has been lovingly cared for. Or that someone extremely knowledgeable went about rehabilitating the antique. The truth is changes were made to it—pieces were glued back together, missing pieces were crafted, the finish was enhanced. Was the piece desirable prior to its conservation? Conserved seems to suggest so but...

The terms *refreshed or restored* are more direct and less euphemistic but despite their directness also obscure. Was the item damaged, why was it "refreshed" in the first place, and was the cleaning or repairs major or minor? Does the marketplace or a fellow collector approve of the refreshment?

Deaccessioned accurately describes a piece that has been removed from a museum's holdings and is being placed for sale. If the museum is a noted one, the piece's cachet may rise in collectors' opinions. But "deaccession" says nothing about whether the piece has merit or that the museum does.

Attributed to or *of the circle* of is another example. How strong is the evidence that the piece's attribution has any confidence—baseball bat purportedly swung by Babe Ruth, fountain pen purportedly used to sign the Emancipation Proclamation. And what is the value of the piece if it is of "the circle of" and not by the noted craftsman himself?

Reportedly and *probably* are honest to a degree. The provenance as to craftsman, circa date, location, or previous ownership is not certain. But to what degree do reportedly or probably refer? Is the piece 95% certainty of being 18th century or 5%, is it very likely the piece was owned by the duke, or a rumor fed by whispers? Attribution even if uncertain seems better than no attribution at all, but is it?

Provenance issues seem to imply that ownership of the piece, often works of art, has missing gaps or is simply unclear. But it also is a way of saying the piece may have been stolen or looted. Euphemisms are wonderful, aren't they?

Bought out of the house purports to fill in any missing gaps by suggesting that a piece was purchased from the family of the original owner centuries ago. That is true of some pieces, and the provenance typically adds to their value. But for other pieces it simply was purchased from a house, apartment, condo, and the like. The term suggests strong provenance but only suggests it. A collector is well served to do his due diligence.

Evocative may be used to describe an antique in which its

emotional impact is emphasized, while other positive qualities are unmentioned as are craftsmanship deficiencies.

Discovered is a term collectors may encounter for a piece that was unknown or lost to the Americana world and seems to imply positive attributes and good monetary value. It has a mysterious ring to it, promising a good story behind the piece's entrance to the sunlight once again. But aren't many pieces discovered? Isn't that what a country auction down a narrow country road with several generations of belongings is all about?

Well loved, such as a teddy bear, table or chair is a way of saying that the piece is worn or has condition problems. It may lead a collector to believe or be proud that despite wear and tear, or outright damage that the piece is still desirable, charming, and attractive.

Relic or *Survivor* connotes a piece that is to be treasured. But many collectors would respond: "I cannot believe someone did not throw it out decades or centuries ago." The terms relic or survivor sound learned. But aren't all antiques survivors in their own way?

Unique, Rare, or *One-of-a-Kind* suggests both scarcity and desirability. But while the terms such as "unique form" may be an accurate description of an antique it again says nothing about the piece's style and connoisseurship qualities. The piece may be a knockout yet sometimes the term really is communicating: "There isn't another one out there like this because no one wanted or asked a craftsman to make such an ugly piece of ____" (fill in the blank). Or the craftsman made two, they sat in his workshop or shop for years, and he moved on to what would sell. Perhaps three collectors in the Americana community would go head-to-head at auction to own the piece; perhaps not three collectors in the entire world would care about it.

Then there exists the term *generous proportions, immense*

or *monumental* which truly can be euphemisms for big, large, appearance challenged, ungainly, and so forth. Many antiques be they furniture or paintings have a size that is pleasing to the eye. A banquet table may have excellent proportions and be immense. But some antiques so labeled are out of proportion and lose their appeal. Can a case piece of furniture be obese?

Second-tier, eclectic, or *box lots.* These are the pieces auction houses must clean out—the odds and ends. You cannot tell that to a consignor directly. So, a euphemism eases the way. The antiques have value but not a great deal. For example, they are not worthy of being included in an auction catalog. As Davis and Richmond described in *Pump Up the Volume* (*Maine Antique Digest*, May 2023) these pieces are the "lesser stuff." They are the "common, the rough, and the bulk." To be honest, they may be *drek.* Harsh words indeed to their owners and thus the euphemisms employed.

Bought well comes to mind. A collector's goal: "bought well" means that a piece went for a fair price or perhaps was a steal. This may be true for good reasons and not be a euphemism at all. Perhaps the collector did his research and knew something about the craftsman or provenance no one else did. Perhaps the piece is part of an estate, and the executor told the auctioneer, "Sell it for what you can, we do not want anything returned to us." Or the seller needs money and will take what he can get.

The story behind our purchase of this piece of redware may be found in the chapter on serendipity. But it truly was bought well. The asking price from the (well known) dealer was below market value (so I thought). I believe I can put it up for auction at a site known for ceramics and make a pretty profit. I can only assume that the dealer himself bought it well and passed on the lower price to us. Sometime a piece truly is a bargain. Both the seller and I were happy.

But the other side of the coin is that the phrase is a euphemism. It could be that the consignor's piece brought a very low bid and sold. "Bought well" is a gentle phrase, much nicer than the seller, for example, got hosed. Of course, if a consignor has multiple pieces at auction, he may do better than he anticipated on others. Bargains have always been part of collecting, and the seller may have purchased a few as well. All's fair in love and collecting.

Keep in mind collectors' responses to euphemisms may be subjective, with differing interpretations. I hope I was not overzealous (too aggressive) or distasteful or candid (insulting) in my presentation of euphemisms. Everyone in the Americana world uses them at one time or another. They can make a collector smile and have an endearing quality about them.

CHAPTER 14

Good Luck

I wait in line for an antique show to open. As the appointed time draws near collectors wish each other "good luck" as they prepare to enter. I do the same. But what exactly is luck?

Luck is success or failure brought about by chance rather than one's actions. To win a lottery is to be lucky. To have a college exam emphasize the only chapter the student read and studied in preparation is lucky. Accidently stumbling upon dinosaur bones is another example. Probability and providence determine the outcome. In collecting American antiques, it may be better to be good (prepared) than lucky. But good luck never hurts.

Do you carry a rabbit's foot or four-leaf clover for good luck? I used to wear the same flannel shirt to all my college final exams, fantastically believing doing so brought me luck. One of my uncles had a silver dollar, worn smooth, when he piloted B-25s in the Pacific in World War II. It was his talisman, and it "worked": He lived to return home. Yet I have no object I believe brings me luck when I bid at auctions or attend shows. Perhaps my collection would be better if I did. Who is to say?

We seem to have a need to believe that what we desire or hope for can be influenced to come to pass. We look for patterns and signs, invoke spirits and gods, making promises to them if they will only help us. People still read their horoscopes to see what the day holds for them. We pray for good fortune. The craps player at Las Vegas looks to the heavens before his throw of the dice. In the movies, the pretty dame accompanying him is responsible for his run at the table. He will not let her leave.

We attempt to account for the randomness of much of life through the concept of luck, assigning patterns or causality to random events. I have no superstitions to assist my collecting, but I imagine that some collectors do.

The need for superstition and gods and goddesses of luck exists because outcomes in real life can be either good or bad. As Franklin Roosevelt wisely observed "I think we consider too much the good luck of the early bird and not enough the bad luck of the early worm."

Luck has been a pervasive concept across cultures and millennia, shaping beliefs, rituals and practices in various ways. Luck was often, and still is, associated with the favor of the gods. The Mesopotamians (west Asia, 8000-2000 BC) believed deities influenced fortune and misfortune. They possessed rituals to appease these gods and secure their favor. In ancient Egypt amulets and charms, such as the ankh and the scarab beetle, were used to solicit protection and good fortune, a long-ago forerunner of my flannel shirt or my uncle's silver dollar.

I look at our collection with a fresh eye. Did luck have a part in our owning this piece or that? I attribute a few pieces (but only a few) in our collection to luck.

A piece of artwork appears to be a prime example: I bid at an auction, and I won the piece in remarkable condition at far less than I expected. Was there no one else interested or who coveted the piece like I did? I think I was lucky. Perhaps competitor collectors were tapped out, or putting their antique dollars towards something else, or were not aware the piece was up for auction. It all worked in my favor, though I did not pray to Mesopotamian gods for their good favor.

I expected several competing bidders at the auction, but I believe there was only one, and she dropped out early. The scene here is a common one and schoolgirls are widely acknowledged for painting it, maybe because it was assigned, perhaps because it is so eye-catching. Nonetheless, I have not seen many paintings like this one, especially in this condition. That Sarah J. Stoddard "signed" and dated her painting (July 18,1843) makes it even more special to me. A fabulous piece of folk-art. I contacted a well-known dealer from whom I had purchased the Chambers and De Grailly paintings. He took a look and liked the painting, telling me that it was worthy of his inventory but if I was going bid on it, he would not. Because competitive bidders were not in evidence the painting has become one of the few "steals" in our collection. It was ours. As an aside, the photograph does not do it justice. It is even better than it shows.

Once I had my success, the adventure and wonderings began. I wondered, "who was she?" Was she a known woman artist? Women artists are highly esteemed and getting their day in the sun. I contacted several dealers in American antiques about which museum to contact to learn more. One dealer sent me to Michael R. and Suzanne Rudnick Payne of New York City, a couple who are known (but were unknown to me) for sleuthing out artists' identities and lives. As I write this, their most recent research is published in the July/August 2024 issue of *The Magazine Antiques*. I heard nothing for a while and then they contacted me. Using various census and other data bases they informed me that there were too many women with the name Sarah J. Stoddard of that period to make headway in identifying her. I was disappointed but at least I had done my research.

This painting also illustrates the confluence of many variables in collecting. It was bought well. It is beautiful. I had my wonderings. Good luck was involved in getting it for the price we paid. It truly was a good buy. Finally, there is a collegiality in the American antique world that is special.

There is one other example in our collection of a piece purchased at a very fair price that probably ought to have gone for more. It is an "ABC" redware plate, the finest I have ever seen. It was purchased at Lewis Scranton's auction (Lewis was a highly esteemed dealer) and it was most affordable. I could have borrowed from the Medieval Period and invoked a saint for good fortune. Or I could have adopted one several Chinese auspicious symbols such as the dragon, phoenix, and the number eight. But none were present, and I invoked neither saint nor Chinese symbols. Yet I was still lucky.

A second type of collector luck is purchasing a piece and unexpectedly and with no hint of such thing being true, have it turn out better than expected. Perhaps a signature is found that no one has discovered, that of a well-known and prized craftsman or limner. It could be that the over-paint on a cupboard is stripped away, and a luscious blue lies underneath, bared for the world to see for the first time in eons.

A jelly cupboard from early in our collector days, purchased over fifty years ago sits near me as I write this chapter. We liked its scale and cutouts on each side of its base. The problem was that it was covered in heavy white paint, so we stripped the paint away. No blue paint underneath but the cherry wood was and is gorgeous—we were lucky.

Did I pray for a wonderful cupboard to any of the ancient

antiquity goddesses?—the ancient Greek goddess Tyche, responsible for fortune and prosperity or to the Roman goddess Fortuna, of luck and fortune? I did not. Perhaps I should in the future to try to tilt luck's presence in my direction once again.

A dealer purchased a strange tallcase clock at auction with a shallow drawer in the base, just above the feet and molding, that would not open. He had never seen such a clock with a drawer. Lying it in his van the drawer opened like Excalibur released from the stone, sliding upward as easily as the day it was made. Laying it on its back had dislodged a jam created by overloaded manila envelopes of genealogy, appraisals, scholarly correspondence, and a catalog of an early exhibition of North Carolina decorative arts which featured, you guessed it, the clock. It was traceable to the original owner, and there was even a speculative assessment on who had made the movement. The clock was then sent to a different auction house where it sold for ten times what the dealer originally paid for it. Lucky indeed.

Another example of this second type of luck is "unexpected authenticity." A collector has purchased a painting, for example, sold as a replica or imitation, no "school of." But it turns out to be the work of a known and respected artist. Someone purchased a "fake" Degas only to have it turn out to be the real thing. No such antiques grace our collection. adding understanding and significance.

A third kind of collector luck is finding a great antique when others have passed it by. The luck lies in the fact that no one has yet purchased it. There is no rhyme or reason why, but dealers often have remarkable pieces in their shops that sit and sit. The blanket chest I talk about in Chapter 31, "Collecting is an Adventure" (that "should" have sold and moved up the "food chain" before my wife and I purchased it from the back of a truck) was seen by thousands. We were lucky it was still for sale. It is pictured in *Come Collect with Me*.

I wonder if this category of luck is "fortune timing"— when a collector is in the right place but accidently also at the right time. We accidently ran into the dealer while most from the show she displayed in had left Manchester (NH).

A fourth type of luck is told and retold by dealers and collectors, stories of being in the wrong place at the right time. How could that treasured antique be found where it was, owned by someone or at auction when it had no right being there? So many American antiques have been found in chicken coops or barns (my wife and I own a Hoadley and Thomas, wooden works tallcase clock found in a barn, pictured in *Come Collect with Me*) as the stories go, that I wonder if these locations are really "wrong," The same is true for American antiques being found in England or other nations far away from where they were crafted. My wife and I have no pieces in our collection we picked from a thrift store or garage sale. If I adopted a Renaissance and Enlightenment mindset, e.g., that astrology and alchemy influenced luck and destiny, and practiced one or both, would the outcome be different? I will let you know in the future.

A fifth type of luck is truly represented by the randomness of life. Sometimes, collectors stumble upon valuable items through unexpected connections or chance encounters with individuals who possess or know about the items they are seeking. These folks are not in the American antique universe. There is one item in our collection that meets this criterion. We owned a "Hoosier cupboard" and wanted a better one. Someone we mentioned this to knew that one was for sale by a friend of theirs. We still have it today.

A sixth type of luck involves gifts or bequests from family or friends. You see this good luck regularly on *Antique Road Show* in both Britain and the States. An antique was inherited or given as a gift by a friend. Lo and behold, it is truly worth something and should be treasured and insured. The reproduction Chinese ancestral portrait discussed in Chapter 28 is one such example.

Have I omitted other types of luck in collecting American antiques? I probably have. But there can be no doubt that good fortune plays a part in collecting American antiques. All that cogitation and categorization aside, an experienced collector believes that he makes his own luck. I check many auction listings. I knew the schoolgirl Hudson valley painting was coming up for auction. Through persistence and hard work a seasoned collector puts himself in situations where the flip of the coin may come up heads (metaphorically) on occasion. The antique is his.

Yet it strikes me that a serious belief in luck makes for the unhappy collector or maybe the careless one: bidding on pieces he has not researched in hopes that the cat will turn out to be a tiger.

Luck has been a constant theme in human history, evolving in its interpretation and significance but always remaining a fundamental part of human culture. Whether viewed through the lens of divine intervention, superstition, or randomness, the concept of luck continues to shape human behavior and societal norms. Each type of luck adds excitement and intrigue to the world of collecting, reminding enthusiasts that sometimes, the most extraordinary finds are the result of chance and circumstance. Good luck to you all.

CHAPTER 15

Marketing

A collector of American antiques is probably so used to it she does not even question anymore. It is as common as iron, oxygen, or helium in the physical world. I speak of marketing—advertisements in trade publications, use of social media including videos of show booths, email blasts to listservs of customers, whispers in show hallways. There may be a photo or two or three, typically in color to show off the antiques at their best. Sometimes it is done the old-fashioned way, via use of the US Mail, even flyers put on telephone poles and bulletin boards.

On a quiet day with my schedule more empty than usual, I began to wonder about the purpose and psychology of all this information. After all, aren't most collectors aware of dealers who handle the genres they collect, of upcoming shows they have attended in the past or plan to attend? Don't most collectors sign up for notifications from auction houses to be reminded of upcoming events? Unfortunately, things do not turn out to be as simple and straightforward as collectors might think.

Let. us leave the world of antiques for a moment. Coca Cola sells two billion(!) servings of Coke a day, yet its marketing is unremitting. They want to keep the name in the public's eye; someone may be coming after them.

I learned that a dealer, auction house or show may market for a broad variety of reasons. For some the goal is to build, enhance or maintain "brand awareness:" "Psst! remember me. I am still here." They want collectors to be aware of the antiques they sell and new arrivals (turnover in inventory). They hope to be more visible, more memorable. A collector with dollars to spend will think of them, or so they hope. On the flip side it is not unusual for a dealer to let it be known "this is what I have sold in the past, and I welcome pieces of this quality or genre to purchase or for consignment." The hints of success and quality are golden. So is the tone, the suggestion that the dealer is speaking with the collector, offering him insights and access.

Such collector awareness is crucial, for new and existing competitors lurk around every corner, just like those unnamed soda-makers. Auction houses spring up with some regularity, surprisingly. Newcomers strive to dislodge a favorite dealer, a cherished and oft-visited show, or a firmly established auction establishment. The buzz of an effective marketing campaign may draw bees to the nectar.

A common marketing goal is to increase sales and revenue. A few months ago, I received an email from a dealer with whom I had dealt in the past. Several color photos with descriptions of items he was bringing to a well-known show were attached. I could not attend the show, but his marketing displayed one piece that I liked, not yet pictured on his website. One thing led to another, and I purchased it. Mission accomplished for this dealer: He had a sale. And the email marketing message and the well-handled exchange helped strengthen our relationship. Such marketing is low cost in both time and dollars, and easy to do. And like me, I am sure many collectors appreciate it.

The basket was the outcome of a simple marketing event used by many dealers. Not the dealer I reference above but another. I received an email from this dealer with several items pictured. The basket was not among them. But I decided to look at the dealer's website. We already owned one small basket purchased years before that my wife liked. On the dealer's website was the basket pictured, an "apple basket" with original green paint. Sandy liked this one too and the price was fair. Had I not received the dealer's email, I believe the basket would have been sold long before I got around to looking at the website sometime in the future. We now own four small baskets so if three truly is the threshold and magic number, we have a collection of them.

The basket is one of many pieces in our collection that are the result of dealer marketing. The Chambers' and DeGrailly painting, the child's chair, the Connie poster in the serendipity chapter, the child's highchair, more than one Black doll in Sandy's collection, among them.

Another goal of marketing is to build demand for a product or service: A part of this effort is image building. A wise dealer reinforces the idea that he cares for his customers, is rock-solid dependable, and has the in that lets him get the best goods. You may not be able to attend a show that his marketing says will have wonderful pieces in his booth, but perhaps the next time you can. An item you truly desire may already be sold, but a dealer with an enticing inventory surely will find a "special antique" to capture your interest, passion, and dollars.

Follow-up to marketing with exceptional service is a must. This is not something put on paper or sent as an email but a necessary effort on the part of the seller. It does the dealer, show, or auction house no good to attract potential or actual customers and then offer them an awful experience. Good relationships with buyers (actual and potential) are important. If successful, with the loyalty built in partly by wonderful service, collectors may purchase again and again from the same dealer, attend the show where he has a booth, or consign to or purchase from the same auction house. The dealer who sent me the email and sold me a wonderful antique mentioned above followed up to see how much I liked it, with a full-page photo of the item, and a detailed description—a sterling example of good service. Dealers do that sort of thing because they know it pays off in the long run. Many enjoy the happiness in a collector's voice they have created.

In the competitive American antiques' market, marketing can help differentiate one dealer, show or auction house from its competitors. It helps the dealer or house stand out. That is why some auction houses work so hard to acquire first-class collections. Maybe it is the dealer's price, her reputation for standing behind the antique or the entire experience, but no matter: What is important is whether the seller-customer connection rings true, chimes sweetly and lingers in memory. A good word about a transaction to other collectors, a compliment regarding courtesy and care; these are the lifeblood of successful purveyors of American antiques.

Besides awareness, interest, and forming positive relationships, marketing also can inspire anticipation. Auction houses and shows want collectors psychologically involved, eagerly looking forward to the event, with plans to add to their collections.

A dealer or auction house may also be trying to expand into new markets. Auction houses typically let people know when they open an office in a new location. I know of at least one dealer who may be the only American antique dealer at one show he takes part in each year. He is surrounded by antiques, jewelry, and artworks that are not Americana. I have been told he does quite well.

Wouldn't you want to do business with an industry leader, all things being equal? Marketing can attempt to establish, promote (and sometimes allege) leaders in the American antique universe. Thus, some auction houses show pieces in ads and publicize the high prices they brought. The message is simple: We can get the most for the good pieces we put on the market. Some dealers on their websites have a button for "prior sales," doing the same. Full page ads in trade publications, especially in prestigious locations (inside front cover, near the front) communicate that this is an important dealer. Perception is after all, reality. If you believe the dealer handles only the "best," you are more likely to upgrade your collection by working with him. Running ads in the same location time after time is an example of "consistent branding." The dealer's logo, typography and photo placement create a visual identity.

Providing important information either through detailed catalogues (dealer or auction house), blogs, webinars or in-person forums on specific topics is another way to demonstrate knowledge and expertise, thus (hopefully) gaining trust and credibility with the target audience. One well-known dealer who has had a shop for decades every so often offers collectors the opportunity to learn about a specific topic. These forums bring collectors to the shop, allowing the dealer to sharpen the knowledge of collectors who may then appreciate (even more) the wares offered, while letting the dealer share his love for his craft, the area he loves so, and the pieces he cherishes.

Marketing also allows dealers, shows, and auction houses to adapt to and read changing customer preferences. Letting it be known that "I (we) now handle mid-century modern or Asian pieces, adding these genres to our expertise and wares," can shift the buyer base and expand it. The Winter Show in New York City that used to have many dealers in American antiques now has only a few because trends, interests and buyer commitments are always subtly shifting. To survive, the show had to adapt and change. Marketing brings these changes to collectors' attention.

Marketing in all its forms needs engaging content. I recently reread a year's worth of *Maine Antique Digest* with an eye towards finding interesting and inviting adver-tisements and frequently found them. It is one reason, I believe, *MAD* is so much fun to read. (Full disclose—I may be biased because of my sunk costs. I have been a subscriber almost since *MAD* first appeared.) I find that the ads are visually appealing and match the color photos of auctions and shows in quality and interest.

Some in the American antique world probably market too little. The collector finds herself saying, "Why didn't I know of him or them before?" Some may market too much, leading to what is called "fatiguing your audience." "Enough already," the collector says. Just like Goldilocks and the Three Bears, dealers, auction houses and shows strive for the sweet spot, not too little and not too much.

A common marketing mistake is to mislead the intended audience. The goods look wonderful in the color ad in a trade publication but most of the pieces up for auction are not that good or are not even Americana at all. It is the equivalent of food photography: How can I resist that stacked hoagie showing tomato, onion, cheese, and the dealer's "special sauce"?

Anyone who markets in the American antique world must understand his target audience. Failing to understand the preferences, tastes, and interests of it may lead to campaigns that do not resonate with the intended buyers.

Many do a stellar job marketing, serving the collector or consignor. Let us not underestimate the marketing of American antiques in assisting collectors in building their collections. We acquire knowledge and understanding about the market, train our eyes, and know what is for sale and coming up for sale to name just three.

There are those (maybe that is too dismissive) who have convinced themselves they can live without advertising, that marketing is lie piled on lie, that words and images exaggerate. If you are a collector, picture pursuing your passion without information, comparisons or an idea of the market. As a matter of fact, advertising serves a purpose estranged from the seller: It is a valuable, informational tool, which may be why the science—oft changed, sometimes salted with egregious fictions—has been around for so long. Caution, even suspicion, is not out of place, but the wise collector uses the ads as yet another source for her research. Ignore marketing at your peril.

Learning about marketing made me appreciate the various reasons, dealers, shows, and auction houses go about their business—and why some, already highly prestigious and known to all (or almost all) keep their name prominently in the collector's eye. If I was such a dealer, for example, I would take great pleasure in tasteful ads with wonderful antiques bearing my name or the name of my shop. I would take pride in letting the world know of a wonderful piece I have in my possession or have sold in the past.

CHAPTER 16

Seduction and the Casting of Spells

"I just love that highboy! Look at the (portrait) bust. Oh, the lines! Ooh, the legs." "The curves." "Original surface." The very language of antique collecting seems oddly like that of romance (Okay, maybe not original surface.) Marvelous objects entice, ensorcell, enchant, enrapture.

Hardened collectors can be reluctant lovers, yet they often bathe in a pool of wonder, promise, and fulfillment and finally drown in the languishing water of "I must have." Harry Potter and King Arthur are twisted about by Hermione and Guinevere until they cannot separate the real from the implied. And so are collectors. Seduction is all around them.

"I'm in the Mood for Love," a 1935 song moans the mood is "Simply because you're near me." But there are other causes for rapture—the classic candlelight dinner with soft music playing in the background, the presence of fine alcohol, Lanvin perfume and muted conversation. One or both participants blissfully await magic in the air, the same spell that entraps collectors, plunging them into the abyss.

I have never seriously considered seduction and the casting of spells in the collectors' world. If you have not either, prepare to be enlightened, perhaps bewitched.

"I heard words like *sexy*, *beguiling*, and *enigmatic*, being used to describe it..." "Quite simply, the piece seduced all who crossed its path." (*Hidden Treasures: Searching for Masterpieces of American Furniture*, Keno, L. & Keno, L., page 11) "... a number of spotlights dramatically accentuated its form." (page 12) "I hung the chairs from fishing line strung at eye level ... Doing so forced visitors to confront the chairs as sensual, sculptural forms. ..." (page 49) The same tome tells collectors of a table with "chic and poise" and "curves ... movement, ... and sex appeal." It celebrates the "cool beauty of the entire form." This is the Kenos' introduction to the antique as siren.

Objects are described as having "beautiful form," "stunningly sleek form," or "gorgeous." A reporter for *Maine Antique Digest* wrote in disappointment several years ago that collectors at one auction did not go "absolutely bonkers" (act as if bewitched?).

My determined mining of the collector's mentality, language and behaviors strongly suggests we have entered the world of seduction (from the Latin, meaning "leading astray") and the necessary casting of spells. We could be talking about Betty Grable, Errol Flynn, or Rita Hayworth from the golden era of cinema, or the love of my movie life (from afar of course), Lauren Bacall. A compelling woman is a seductress, a siren, a temptress. We need parallel labels for antiques (and dealers) that seduce—the rake, the dandy, the charmer, or the coquette do not seem to do. And what do we call a collector who looks upon an antique with desire? A fool for love (as those CW songs would have it), a willing victim, lucky?

Seduction sometimes involves more than the antiques themselves. Many collectors have experienced such seduction and there are times when they not only endure being seduced but willfully seek it, for there is pleasure in the sin—form, lighting, the soft voice of a dealer. In seducing the collector, the goal is to subtlety tempt him with antiques and incite interest That colonial table cannot be the equivalent of a streetwalker. Wrong, wrong vibe! But the hoarse-voiced beauty with a swath of blond hair shading one eye, yes!

The wooer, if a dealer or auctioneer, also must choose the correct victims, and collectors of Americana fill the bill being susceptible to antiques' charms. Toss in a bit of the exotic (provenance perhaps, or rarity or condition) and behold! the enticing seller and the bemused collector are dancing their dance.

Odysseus had his men fill their ears with wax to avoid the sirens' temptation. Yet he tied himself to the mast so he could hear their irresistible temptation, but live. Many consider him to be the preferred role model for the wise collector who is lured by the siren song of an antique, dealer, or auctioneer, but through will power if nothing else insulated from temptation, at least for the moment.

Listen closely to Casanova who observes and celebrates the wiles of women (and men), who limns the art form needed to get what one wants through allurement and attraction. For our purposes the art of persuading may have sexual overtones, but with the end goal of the buying and selling of antiques! The art of seduction can be innocuous or immoral, but collectors experience it all the time and oft enjoy it.

What made Lauren Bacall seductive? Her deep throaty voice for one. And her signature look—chin down with eyes peering seductively upwards—has been often imitated but never matched. Her blond hair, her "you can't have me" demeanor. And of course, some of the lines she said or purred: "You know you don't have to act with me, Steve." (*To Have and To Have Not*) While antiques cannot talk in words, they do communicate. Put those elements together and you have one alluring woman or highboy, take your pick.

Seduction in all its complexity can involve an indirect and subtle use of scent, sight, words spoken, and gestures unspoken, things common in collecting environments. The antique is presented as an object of desire, sometimes in a praiseworthy disguise. The seller pretends the piece is just a Thing, only a chair, perhaps. Just as for Odysseus, temptation is everywhere. The object flirts with the collector, its messages are suggestive. "Look at me." "I want you to want me." "If you do not desire me someone else will." "You know you have always wanted me." The collector gazes, the collector touches. The collector thinks, "You'd be so nice to come home to."

The object, its setting, the dealer, each in their own way speak of the pleasure of taking "me." One thinks of the holiday song "Baby It's Cold Outside." "I have to go home," the collector says," "Please stay," the antique responds, but not too assertively.

It was early in our collecting days, 1977 to be exact. A dealer had a reproduction painting of Smutt the Cat. Smutt may well be the most famous folk-art cat. He was painted in circa 1870 by an unknown artist and is a gorgeous tiger. As cat lovers we were smitten, more than smitten, enraptured and captured. We had to have Smutt, and the price was reasonable. An article from March 1987 in *Antique Review* stated that "'Smutt the Cat' had adorned the cover of the catalogue for the 1976 exhibition at the Museum of American Folk Art, *American Cat-alogue: The Cat in American Fok Art*. At Sotheby's in 1987, with an estimate of $30,000 to $40,000 he was adored to the extent of $55,000. "Seduced by a cat?" you say. We were easy fodder for Smutt and have adored him ever since.

Interestingly, we subsequently never pursued period paintings of cats over the years. We have the rogue's gallery of cats we have owned over the decades painted in folk-art style. That has satisfied us. But Smutt is special. We did have our wonderings (see Chapter 6). I had never pursued information on his artist, Norma Berry. In writing this vignette, I was motivated to find her and located her 2012 obituary. She was "a teacher, artist and ran an antique shop with her husband. She studied at the National Academy of Art in NYC, the Art Students League of NY and holds a degree of Fine Arts from SU. She was ... a member of the Cazenovia Watercolor Society and the Central NY Pastel Society." I learned that pieces we have owned for decades still have stories to tell.

Where is Smutt? I could not find him at the American Folk-art Museum or the Metropolitan Museum of Art.

Clayton Pennington, Editor of *Maine Antique Digest* nor his staff knew. David Schorsch who has a long history as a dealer in the American antique world and has handled many high-end paintings also did not know. I asked the question, "Where is Smutt?" on social media and put in a request in *Maine Antique Digest* but Smutt remains hidden. Perhaps he will resurface someday.

A high-end antique show meets our criterion of seduction, and rather well. It provides "pretty people and pretty things need to be seen." (Objects of Desire, page 3) On opening night or the show's first full day, muted conversations focused on "have you seen X's charming Y?" float in the air. Champagne helps, as does the glittering array of people at opening night (for which they have paid handsomely). Throw in luxurious carpeting, creative booth designs, spotlights and soft music, and a mood that showcases the wonderful antiques each dealer has subtly slides into place.

After the high-end preview, the bewitching ambience often diminished or gone (poof!) in the light of day. But antiques can cast their own spell, just by being what they are. A beautifully painted Shaker chest needs little assistance to catch and stun the eye, a Philadelphia tea table, no assistance to capture the caress. I remember the Riverside show in Manchester, held in the Armory, a place that should have been looming and hollow. Yet even when largely empty of collectors the setting cast a spell. The pieces spoke, cried out, called for a look, a touch. Outdoor shows also can have their witchcraft—an idyllic day with a blue sky, a warm breeze, and a few puffy clouds.

What does it mean to be under a spell? Typically, the possessed person is so transported and charmed that rational thought is cast away. He acts as if in a daze, aware of what is happening, perhaps, but not in control of his actions. He obeys the will and power of the incantation, of the one who cast the spell. He is enchanted, described as bewitched ("bonkers" at an auction?). Shakespeare's use of a love potion in *A Midsummer Night's Dream* shows the power of bewilderment, the inability to separate fact from illusion, the depth and shallowness of attachments and the magic of not knowing the difference.

Incantations in the American antique universe? The dealer's abracadabra may be his detailed knowledge of the genre this piece represents so well, creating desire in the antique's uniqueness, specialness, or alluring lines. The collector feels it can be hers I'm in the mood ... the collector feels. And without imbibing Love Potion Number 9 she is suddenly besotted.

The three witches in Shakespeare's *Macbeth* influence the decisions he makes, convincing him to desire the crown and then trick him into a suicidal fight. While he made the decisions that determined his fate, they lead him to his eventual destruction. The witches controlled his mind, but it was his own free will that makes MacBeth the tragic figure he is. It is no less true for the collector.

The spell on the audiences that movies cast to make the Lauren Bacalls of the cinema bewitching depended on such stars having that undefinable "something" that acting alone cannot produce. A chemistry between them and costars, and them and the audience existed and was sustained. Just like with fine antiques. But sometimes it is as Cole Porter wrote (1935), "Just one of those things," and the antique that so seduced, by morning's light is ordinary. The collector has indeed been led astray. "It was just one of those nights."

What spirits do collectors or antiques invoke before an auction or show? What spells do MacBeth's witches bestow on collectors? All collectors cherish certain images inside their imaginations, for example, the perfect folk-art painting of the Hudson from West Point (see Chapter 14). When an external object meets a collector's internal expectations the sparks fly. Do collectors even know they are being seduced? Do they care? Most of the time, I think not.

CHAPTER 17

Serendipity

Chance favors the prepared mind.
Louis Pasteur,
French chemist, microbiologist, and inventor

Collectors sometimes find that it is the unplanned moment that rises in importance. I think of happenstance, a random event that happens by chance or coincidence. A wonderful word, happenstance, a combination of happen and circumstance, originating in America in the middle to late 19th century. Some would lean towards *serendipity*, unsought, unintended, and/or unexpected events; it is a fortunate discovery and/or learning experience that happens by accident.

Serendipity also has a wonderful history. The word was coined by Sir Horace Walpole, Earl of Oxford, in the 1700s. He used the word to define "accidental discoveries." In a letter to a friend, Walpole wrote about "The Three Princes of Serendip," a somewhat silly fairy tale. "*... as their highnesses travelled, they were always making discoveries, by accidents and sagacity, of things which they were not in quest of.*" What is Serendip but the old name for Ceylon, Sri Lanka). The tale described three princes' fates who had left home to travel the world. Whereas they rarely found the treasures they sought, they encountered others they were not seeking, often even greater.

Some would describe such events as the operation of fate, others as that of the hand of God. Whichever you consider, I believe that being prepared looms large role in these "accidental" goings on. Serendipity is not luck per se, but chance interacting with a prepared mind. Collecting then is not only a matter of logic, reading and study. A collector must be prepared but also predisposed to act. Unexpected events may present opportunities, if seen as such. In other words, collecting is more than being in the right place at the right time. It is the response to the perceived opportunity, the sagacity of the collector and his willingness to act that makes serendipity not only so important but more likely.

Serendipity played a role in what we now take for granted: vaccination, insulin to treat diabetes, vulcanized rubber, and quinine. Many basic discoveries—Velcro, Teflon, microwave ovens, x-rays, pulsars, and radioactivity—were due to serendipity. The Nobel Prize (first awarded in 1901) exists because of Alfred Nobel's wealth and values. What you may not know is that he "accidently" discovered dynamite.

Pasteur's observation regarding chance may be deeper than it seems on first observation. What he is saying is that we have some control and bear some responsibility in making luck. Being successful is more than chance. If we are successful, the universe is telling us to keep on the road we are traveling, to keep going. While we have been waiting for the world to treat us favorably, the world has been waiting for us.

All of which is relevant to the world of Americana and its collectors who are repeatedly told to "be prepared." Serendipity supports this maxim. It is the collector with a prepared mind who succeeds. Such a collector is not only the recipient of good fortune but is an active participant in it. To be more direct once again, one might say that "he knows his stuff." For what lies behind serendipitous moments or discoveries is a lot of hard work and toil. These are sustained by passion and in turn develop a keen and sharp mind. Often attributed to Thomas Jefferson but probably better to anonymous, an insightful, humorous quote says: "I'm a great believer in luck, and I find the harder I work the more I have of it."

The serendipity pattern appears rather simple. X finds Y. X knows what he has in hand because (1) he is knowledgeable about the field, (2) he knows what a decent price is ... and what he had in his pocket, and (3) he has been in the right place at the right time. In the first two examples that follow the collector can control the outcome. The third is happenstance. I say "appears rather simple" because it takes a great deal of hard work and preparation to be in the right place at the right time and *take advantage of the circumstances.*

My wife and I are on vacation in northern Michigan, the UP to Yooper natives. We are driving its back roads and come upon a small town, one of many in the region, just a happenstance on our roadway, with a retail district two blocks long. A small bookstore beckons, a treasure box waiting to be opened, though we do not know that. My wife immediately goes to the young adults' section looking for works about girls or women who fly. Lo and behold, she holds up a tome. As I stand in the next aisle with my mouth open, she rummages in her purse and pulls out a list of books in her collection. She does not own the work she clutches in her hand, and we purchase it. It is her preparedness that allows her to do with confidence. Given its relatively affordably she probably would have bought it even without her list, but the sense of triumph would have been lost, replaced by uncertainty. Serendipity personified for we could have taken any number of roads and discovered other small towns save this one, and she had no inkling this particular volume was anywhere within her orbit, not only in a minute village but in the distant Upper Peninsula.

In another instance I check my email, and there is a photo of a piece of redware from a known dealer (pictured in Chapter 13). The slip reads, "money wanted," and the platter has slip across almost all of it. The condition is excellent except for one gouge. The email was sent by a dealer-friend who was attending the York, Pennsylvania show, and the piece was for sale by a dealer I was aware of but had never purchased from. I call the dealer's cell, and the conversation goes something like this:

"Hi, a friend sent me a photo of a piece of redware in your booth that says, 'money wanted.' Do you still have it for sale?"

"Yes," he says.

My heart skips a beat. "Can you tell me its condition and what you are asking for it?"

"I'll go get it," he says. He returns to the phone in a minute or two. "The condition is excellent except for the gouge and the price is X. He names a price that is half again or even less of what I thought he would quote. An excellent deal for a rare saying I tell myself."

"I am thinking of having the gouge repaired," I tell him.

"We think alike," he responds. "The dealer next to me at the show does that, and it would increase, not decrease the value of the platter."

"What does such repair work cost?" I ask. He tells me, and it is most affordable.

We strike a deal. I have never attended the York show. I did not know he had the platter for sale until I received the photograph from my friend. I knew the market and my expectation of the asking price for the platter was based on past sales. I know that redware can be repaired and hence my question. I have found a bargain. Perhaps more importantly I have a dealer new to me with whom to develop a relationship for he has more. One might say the platter appeared out of the blue but while I was waiting for the world, it was waiting for me. Again, my preparedness—knowledge of the genre and market prices allow serendipity to improve our collection.

We have a small, but I believe good, collection of aviation posters. They reflect my wife's interest in women who fly, the Pan Am Clipper, the trimotor, and the Women Airforce Service Pilots (WASPs). One of the jewels reflects her love for the Lockheed Constellation, affectionately known as "Connie," a propeller drive, four-engine bird that debuted in 1943. One or two still flying. Many, and we are among them, consider Connie the most beautiful airliner ever produced and put into service.

We have seen Connie sitting on the tarmac, but in Oshkosh at the EAA (Experimental Aircraft Association) convention—12,000 planes on the ground and at The Museum of Flight at Boeing Field in Seattle—and she seduced us. Fate was to roll the dice. When visiting an online show, an image of Connie stopped me in my tracks. Neither my wife nor I knew this image even existed: the Connie flying into New York City (lower Manhattan) at dusk, the city alit and the Statue of Liberty with its torch afire. "Flying is the way to Travel—and TWA is the way to fly." I showed the image to my wife. She was as bewitched as I.

As chance would have it, the poster was in the booth of a dealer one of our sons and we have purchased from before. The poster was in "A" condition, the colors amazingly fresh. Eventually the deal was closed. It now sits upstairs in our home, and I continue to look for a place to view it every day. It is one of the few pieces of art we own that would prompt me to rearrange all that we have on display, to make it more prominent.

What a wonderful example of serendipity. I expected to find nothing at the show but felt I should look; a collector should always look. We had trusted ourselves in rejecting previously an image of Connie we liked but did not love in the hope that someday a more desirable, moving example would be united with us. That hope was realized purely accidently. But in reading this chapter you know that is truly not so. Chance truly favors the prepared.

This poster is yet another example of the confluence of characteristics and influences in collecting. Serendipity certainly played its part. But had we not been bewitched by the mage we would not have purchased the TWA poster. Finally, as Chapter 19 emphasizes, collectors build collections that reflect who they are. It makes little sense for a house full of high-country antiques to have a sub-collection on aviation, but ours does. We would have it no other way.

Another story. A well-known dealer visits a prestigious show after the hordes of collectors have emptied it of what are supposedly the really desirable pieces. He finds a piece of furniture he very much likes and purchases it. As he sits in the booth talking with the dealer from whom he bought it, he mentions in passing that he is looking for first-class smalls to purchase. "Oh my god," says the dealer-seller. "I have a piece in a highboy I forgot to put out." He rummages in the highboy and produces a wonderful William and Mary mirror which his dealer-customer purchases on the spot. Had the dealer-customer not purchased the piece of furniture, or mentioned in passing what he was looking for, and the dealer-seller not suddenly remembered the piece he had forgotten to display which well may have sold by then, had it been visible in his booth, the mirror would never have gone home with our protagonist. Such is the nature of serendipity.

As you expect, or already know from your own collecting, many of us in the Americana universe experience serendipity. The auctioneer who looks behind a door or in a dresser while on a home visit and finds a painting that had no business being where it was and in fine condition still. And more.

I have presented three personal examples of serendip-ity, and others. I guess that makes them a collection. Finding antiques due to serendipity often makes for some of the warmest memories and best stories a collector has in his rep-ertoire. I would very much enjoy hearing your own discoveries that came to you unexpected and out of the blue. Or did they really?

CHAPTER 18

A Week in the Life of a Collector

I am a dedicated collector of Americana, but I had never taken a "deep dive" into what my collecting entails nor have I read about others doing the same. So, for one week I kept track of my collecting behaviors and offer them for your viewing, tossing in a few observations along the way. Let me know how representative my week is if for no other reason, so I learn how "normal" (or not) I am.

An auction house contacts me via its alert function. Two Hubley steel airplanes, circa 1940, give or take a few years, to add to my wife's growing collection, come up for bid soon. One is listed as having almost a dozen followers, which suggests bidding may be heated. I snag them both at a fair price. The entire bidding process online takes less than 5 minutes. I cannot help but admire the amazing algorithms some auction houses use. I am also struck by the additional cost of the omnipresent buyer's premium and shipping. Once I would have reached for my pocket calculator to figure what these purchases cost, but now I easily factor those expenses into my bidding. The auction houses have trained me well.

For some years I have pursued redware with writing and names inscribed in slip. The market is scorching hot. I have recently purchased a *Prudance & temperance* redware platter.

I love the saying, the spelling of *Prudance*, its condition, and its history. Adding it to my collection was a reach financially but I wanted a special piece before prices rose even more. The dealer tells me that shipping is in the offing.

This redware platter truly was "bought well." While it was not inexpensive the dealer's price was one that we thought eminently fair. It is a good example that many pieces fit into more than one category of collector experiences and characteristics. We purchased the platter as agreeable collectors. We also truly loved it. It spoke to us. We had never seen another in the marketplace. The fact it was for sale was surprising. It had belonged to a dealer's father and mother (the dealer is a third-generation antique dealer).

The loaf dish is connected to American history, one reason it is special to us. The American Temperance Society was established in Boston in 1826. The movement gained momentum and by 1834 5,000 local temperance organizations associated with the American Temperance Society were active. Perhaps the loaf dish served as a collection plate for a local Temperance Society. According to theological philosophers, Prudence and Temperance were recognized as two of the four Cardinal Virtues (Justice and Fortitude the other two). The loaf dish captures an important moment of growth for the Temperance Movement in America.

The day or two after the purchase I have a bigger grin than when I bought the platter, a sure sign of a good decision. The joy of collecting often lies in the anticipation. Oh, the plate itself will furnish day-to-day delight, but there are other factors—I include that misspelling and the realization that we have preserved something with historical importance.

It is near the end of the year, so several January auctions are scheduled, including the high-end ones at Sotheby's and Christie's in New York City. I would very much like to find a piece I crave at one of these auctions that I can afford and lo and behold Bill DuPont's collection has a couple of affordable smalls I have my eye on. I already have corresponded with a friend who badly wants a piece that he underbid in 2010. The experience reminds me how much of being a collector involves a sense of community. Over the years I have become friends with a broad range of fellow aficionados, some with passions for objects that leave me unstirred, all of whom are sources of fascination.

One of the DuPont pieces is a pair of Philip Syng Jr., Circa 1750, Philadelphia sugar nips. I research prices for similar pieces by the same maker and find one pair online sold by a dealer and several pairs by different makers—including two on eBay, of all places. Since I do not consider myself a "serious collector of silver" (yet) I can easily walk away if the price climbs beyond what I have decided is my limit.

What am I willing to pay? The collector's dilemma. The collecting process tells you about your limits. Note that I 'stretched" my budget for the redware plate I love, but suddenly I am charier about spending when it comes to sugar nips, about which my feelings are less elevated.

I am receiving daily photos on social media from still another auction house. The marketing is intense and unremitting. I understand the beneficial and common-sensical reasons for marketing yet at the same time, I feel a bit under siege, and the barrage of postings wants me to say, "enough." There can be decreasing return of scale when marketing, i.e., the message can become counterproductive. I wonder if I am not alone in my feelings. The ubiquity of social media has rendered selling into an ever-present irritant. Of course, you need not be a collector to realize this. I have never seen a discussion of collectors' responses to the marketing we receive. Lordy! Another item for my to-do list. (See chapter 15 for my initial discussion of marketing.)

I look at the online catalog, and I find one small I might consider. The fact is that many collectors do not proceed in straight lines. It would seem perfectly logical for me to mumble. "I just got those sugar nips; now I should buy a silver sugar bowl." In fact, my next buy just might be a cast-iron biplane, a Windsor chair, or a wonderful weathervane. What catches my interest in not only interesting but somewhat unpredictable? And I suspect I am not alone.

I want a carved curlew, and a new one will do. See what I mean? Our three windowsills in the dining room have carved birds sitting on them and a windowsill in the adjacent living room calls out for another. (The curlew call is a harsh whistled cur-lee, rising on second note. This call is given year-round. They also give a rapid whistled tremolo with a slight stuttering quality to it.) A dealer friend has one in his collection—not for sale—that I love, and he sends me a photo that I post on several different social media group pages. I ask if a craftsman can make one like it for me. Amazingly, I get no takers. A lesson learned but I am not sure what the lesson is. I contact a dealer I know who specializes in antique decoys but also sells new ones.

Tis the holiday season and time for me to polish our coin silver. I am reminded of the television series, *Upstairs Downstairs* that aired from 1971 to 1975 with a sequel in 2010. Clearly, my habits, not to mention my income, would have sentenced me to residing downstairs. I have my polishing routine down and all pieces receive the same loving care. The pieces gleam and shine, motivating me to perhaps purchase additional pieces, like the sugar nips I fantasize owning. Had I known how much I like silver today, I would have collected more in the past decades. But I can still see what is available and perhaps snag a piece or two in the months and years ahead. Despite growing older there is always time for a collector to add to his holdings.

Maine Antique Digest is available online. I have the paper issue sent via first class mail too, so I get an early look at ads and features in both formats. I look forward to the print version and curling up with it. (Full disclosure. I have subscribed to MAD forever and enjoyed it immensely, long before I began contributing to it.)

Despite the endless public kvetching about the USPS, the post office delivers the issue of *MAD* in record time by today's standards. A mug of tea in hand, I begin my ritualized reading. It is not unusual for me to read about an item at auction or a show I might have bid on or been interested in had I known it existed, but there are few regrets. Had I been interested in a piece; the final price very well could have been higher as the final buyer, and I bid back and forth. I only had one or two moments of humming "If I were a rich man..." There is also *The Bee* (*Antiques and the Arts Weekly*) that I receive online each week. Another slice of heaven.

An idea is forming in my head, always a dangerous occurrence. One of the auctions in January has two small redware banks, three or four inches high. Another auction has one such bank. I have often thought of owning a few but have never pursued them. Do I want more small objects in the house? How would they look if grouped? And if they were ever truly used as banks, how did folks get their coins out of them once placed within? I learn people would break them open or enlarge the area around the coin slot. Does that mean that unvandalized small redware banks are relatively rare? I learn they are not, but something about them still attracts me.

A timed online auction is posted, and I am relieved there is nothing that interests me. I have never seen anything written about my feeling of relief, but I cannot be the only collector who has a piece or two on the horizon coming up at auction he might want if the price is right, and who is fatigued from keeping track of the various auction offerings and dealers' wares. A strange feeling to smile at the knowledge there is at least one auction to cross off my list. Who knew finding nothing could be construed as a victory? Oh, the irony.

I am amused by my relief that there is nothing more to covet (for the moment). How many pieces can a collector fall in love with at the same time? I am a collector better suited to dining on the extensive menu one piece at a time, a more leisurely style, compared with those who like a lot of action with hard fought opportunities. Striking out at an auction or two simplifies my thinking and lets me focus on where I truly want to spend my antique dollars.

My feelings of comfort and solace, rather than disappointment, means that I am tired, going at collecting a bit too hard.

When this "condition" strikes me, I know from experience that I am likely to make buying mistakes, both of commission (buying something I normally would have probably passed on) and of omission (missing an item I normally would have pounced on). As the week draws to a close it is time to take a break. I practice as best I can what I preach in Chapter 22 about quitting.

So how did things turn out? *The Prudance & temperance* redware platter arrived and is safely ensconced in the corner cupboard in our living room. It is already one of my favorite antiques. I won the single redware bank, estimated at $400 to $600, and paid more than that; I decided I very much liked the form and glaze. I dropped out of the bidding on the other two. With the sugar nips coming up later in the auction I decided to save my dollars for them. With an estimate of $1,500 to $2,500, they sold for $5,670, a fair price but more than I was willing to pay. My friend did purchase the Delaware tall case clock he wanted so badly and was pleased about both its price and finally owning it. And the dealer who sells decoys, got back to me; he awaits replies from some of his carvers. But nothing panned out, and I shall keep looking.

I must consider the lapsed week a relative success. I have learned a few things about myself—it would be gross denial to say I really understand all my motivations. The redware platter and my wife's Hubleys can be checked off as successes, the passed sugar nips a prudent decision, the possible curlew replica a matter of hope. My newfound realization that there are degrees of my collecting passion, depending on the genre and piece, deserves a bit of study and probing, as does an investigation of how collectors respond to the din of advertising. The unreaped acreage of new offerings just sits there as a challenge. Being a collector takes work. Phew.

Collecting is not only great fun but a never-ending process of waiting, hoping, dreaming, winning, losing. If, as Shakespeare wrote in *As You Like It*, "All the world's a stage/ And all the men and women merely players," then I indeed enjoy the collecting stage and playing upon it. I hope you do also.

CHAPTER 19

Do What You Want to Do

Life is all about choices. Choices made and not made. Turning left or turning right. While we have no choices as to the genes we inherit, we can and do choose how we respond to being short or tall, redhead or brunette, healthy or ill. At times we are forced to endure, at others we seek to remedy. And while sometimes we cannot avoid the hand that we are dealt in life we can choose who we play it with. Choices bring freedom or can seem damning in their complexity. Sometimes choices involve unexpected consequences, positive and negative. Collectors know this lesson all too well.

Hardly anything in our lives, unless we are professional victims, takes shape without our making decisions. The collector is no exception: He must be knowledgeable about the marketplace as well as the genre he collects. American antiques have their own history: fitness to their era, levels of craftsmanship, even (one hates to say this) fads and fancies. So many unacknowledged powers influence the attractiveness, availability and value of antiques that falling back on chance and wishfulness to shape one's choices seems and is foolhardy. Collectors need to be aware of and sensitive to the world to successfully collect Americana.

Collectors can take the road less traveled or ride with the

crowd. They can follow whatever rules of thumb they like, purchase the genres they choose, and spend what they opt to when doing so. Fellow collectors may support and approve of their decisions or may look askance. But in the end, it is their collection, and they are free to do as they choose. My wife and I collect American antiques. French ones you might say —never. But you would be in error.

Certainly, our collection of airplane posters, toy airplanes, and Sandy's collection of works of fiction about women who fly reflects our interests. But it is not what one would expect necessarily from collectors of high-country Americana. Pictured is one outlier among several in our collection. The small Jaspe ware pitcher is French, not American. We own only one other French antique, a group of pewter tablespoons purchased long ago. As I write this, we are replacing their display with three American coin silver serving spoons, though we will keep the French ones out of habit and affection, and out of sight.

But the French pitcher we will keep, proudly displayed on a shelf in the kitchen. We love its small size, the out-of-shape mouth (opening) when viewed from above, and its glaze. We did not intentionally set out to buy a French antique or a pitcher of its size, but when we saw it, we both immediately knew we liked it. After all, "do what you want to do."

As a collector I have learned that while choices may bring collectors joy and pleasure, they also carry with them angst, for there is no one correct way to go about collecting. Let us not look at the freedom of choice as always empowering and a good thing. The wide variety of choices collectors face can be overwhelming if they are even aware of them and, if so, dwell on them for too long. For good reason most collectors do not overthink the multitude of decisions open to them. To do so would be formidable and counterproductive.

The paradox of choice is that having too many makes choosing difficult and can lead to "analysis paralysis." Do I collect 17th, 18th or 19th century pieces? What style of furniture, paintings, clocks if any, ceramics, or boxes? Decisions may be delayed or avoided, or obversely, made impulsively. Yet there is always the moment when a collector must pull the trigger. That is why being knowledgeable is important and being cautious, at least most of the time, even more so.

"Bad" choices must be discussed. The gent who wanders into a junk shop thinking it is an antique shop is likely to overspend for whatever he buys, imagining that 1940s Zippo lighter he sees as a bargain when it is really a Japanese knock-off punched out of a Pabst Blue Ribbon can. The collecting horse needs reins: enough background study to ascertain authenticity, enough self-control to let sense precede enthusiasm, and enough perspective to know yourself. Miss any of the three and a collector is most likely to make bad decisions.

Awareness of the breadth and depth of decisions available to collectors can induce stress, as they worry about what to decide and the wisdom in that choice. Collectors may second guess their choices and feel regret. "Was there a better choice I could have made?" A plethora of choices may make it challenging for a collector know which decisions are most important and have the highest priority. One hates to state the obvious, but the transparency of an act does not make it less valuable. Thus, after-the-fact deliberations are almost always the father of anxiety. The better informed a collector's choice is, the less stress he will probably suffer.

The truth is that collectors are free to choose however they like (although hidden, subtle, and unknown influences may affect the decisions they make). Did they fall in love with American furniture, or when they saw nautical paintings, knowing they had to have one, and then a few? Perhaps a dealer early in their collecting career schooled them in painted tin or blanket chests, redware or coin silver, American flags, or Hudson Valley or nautical paintings. At that point in their lives, they were drawn to these or other genres and objects and began to build a collection. For some the collection is a reminder and legacy of mom or dad. Another dealer, another genre, a different itch twenty years ago would have resulted in a wholly unrecognizable hoard—say Batman comics instead of 18th century chairs.

I present myself as an example of what can happen: Only relatively recently did I begin to covet Hudson Valley paintings. I am somewhat surprised by this, even though I have always loved the water and when younger owned several contemporary paintings of boats or water scenes. Had I been smitten by views of the Hudson 30 years ago might I have a wall of them? A question with really no answer but only "maybes" or "perhaps." For there are no rules for what genres we collect, and when we do so in our collecting lives, no correct answers, only rules of thumb and our own instincts and preferences as collectors.

Yes, choices can lead to dilemmas. A collector is saving his dollars for a nice piece of redware (with writing on it). He is proud of his small collection of pieces and wants to add to it. A sampler recently caught his attention, yet his collection contains no such examples. Purchasing the sampler would mean delaying adding to his redware for a year or more. As another collector said who faced the same dilemma with a different genre, "It [the piece] would be a real outlier."

But outliers are not by definition out of the question, are they? "How steadfast should anyone be in his collecting?" the same collector asked me. The sampler would be a "collection of one." It might complement other pieces in his collection. How often does a collector deviate from his collecting plan that has served him well, and when he does, what is the outcome? How does he decide?

A good question that deserves an answer. I know, nothing can be said definitively, but something can be said: The collector is not an automaton but a person, and human beings—as everything in this volume testifies—can be led and can choose. A wealth of knowledge ought to be praised and endorsed, but so should powerful admiration of fine craftsmanship. People stray beyond their boundaries, and the effect is often delight.

Adages aid in collectors' decisions. For example, "Do not purchase something because it is a bargain." I do not mean finding an antique at a very low price and snapping it up or then selling it for a profit but purchasing a piece to live with simply because it is good value for the money. Do collectors break the rule, and how does that work out? The only way to find out would be to do so. Rules are made to be broken, aren't they? But such rules exist for a reason, don't they?

Another dictum in collecting any genre comes to mind: "Buy the best you can afford." The reasons are easily understood. Such pieces have the potential to be good or excellent examples, easier to live with and love, dare I say be better "investments?" They have the potential to make a collector's heart sing, something a more mundane (less expensive) piece might not do.

As is true of many collectors, I can "stretch" when I really love a piece and have done so. Our Roberts wooden works tallcase clock (pictured in *Come Collect with Me*) and purchased long ago is one such example. As is the piece that graces that book's cover—a drop front desk. Yet if I was to always buy the best that I can afford I would probably only buy a piece every couple of years, or even less frequently. "What fun is that?" I ask. "Does that make sense?" I have always wondered, what "afford" means in the real world of collectors? A nuanced discussion is needed about "buy the best ..." and I would love to read or hear one. (Another topic for me to think about.) Such deliberations would assist in my collecting decisions.

Of course, the entire issue of buying the best a collector can afford is easily solved if she specializes in genres where the best is financially reachable. But we are back to where this essay began. You can collect whatever and however you like. And an affordable genre may never have appealed to this collector or that. The fact a collector can do as he pleases is one reason that collecting is so challenging and so much fun, and a serious heartache and headache now and then.

Does a collector keep a "mistake" or two just as a reminder? Up to him. I have kept a painted tin teapot (also pictured in *Come Collect with Me,* whose condition is "meh" as a reminder to buy pieces that are better examples of their genres. Does a different collector keep a few of the first pieces he purchased, even if he has better examples in his collection? The schoolhouse clock that graces our den wall has been with us forever and is one such example. Does a collector keep duplicates because these examples are difficult to find? Her choice. Does a collector mix modern and American antiques from two hundred years ago? It depends. To paraphrase the Isley Brothers, "collecting's your thing, do what you wanna do."

A doyen of the antique world addressed these personal preference (choice) questions decades ago.

The selection depends entirely on the individual. Antique furniture is like pease porridge: some like it hot, some like it cold. Some prefer ornateness, others for utter simplicity. Some like early styles, some like late; some like pine, some like satinwood. And the cherished possessions of some are totally undesired by others. (Alice Winchester editor of *The Magazine Antiques*, *Living with Antiques*, 1941, (page 11)

In other words, "To each their own." Collectors have the freedom to exercise their own preferences.

Existentialists posit that one way to define a person is as the sum of his choices. Our collections reflect the choices we all have made, reflecting who we are and the experiences that influence our tastes and partialities. (Yet, interestingly, as I have noted, collectors may not be aware of these hidden influences.)

Dr. Seuss said it well. "You have brains in your head/ You have feet in your shoes/ You can steer yourself in any direction you choose. You're on your own, and you know what you know/ And you are the guy who'll decide where to go." That verse captures the essence of collecting. Of course, each collector can decide differently from the collector ahead of him in line waiting for a show to open. And the next collector, and the next, and the next. All these choices are not measured by whether they are true or faultless. They simply reflect where each collector wants to go. Do not let the choices available to you spoil, or even worse, wreak havoc on your collecting experience. Embrace and learn from them. Good luck on your collecting travels and steer (or fly as in our case) in whatever direction you like.

CHAPTER 20

Finds

Finds are a highlight of collecting. Since they have many definitions, gradations, and nuances, I am unsure agreement exists on what one is, but collectors know when such a discovery takes place. To some a find is a treasure a collector discovers unexpectedly. To others who have spent the day going in and out of many shops with no genre in mind, a find may be falling in love with a piece that they did not know existed, coming home with a treasure that stole their hearts. This was the case for a 19th century painting my wife and I found in a dealer's shop during a day of antiquing, painted scene of a Black grandmother playing checkers with her granddaughter. (It is pictured in Chapter 5.)

To still others a find is an antique priced below market value, in other words, a good buy. To some collectors who prowl garage sales, a find might be an antique mixed in among the chaff of baby clothes and little-used exercise equipment. Finds can even appear at auctions. An off-the-beaten-path auction house that seldom carries Americana may have such an antique. A find for some dealers is a miscatalogued piece of Americana at a well-known auction house. (I have been told by more than one dealer this occurrence is more common than the average collector might expect.)

And to still others a find is a piece in "plain sight," available to all, on a dealer's website or in a shop for months that others have passed by. The piece languishes and then a collector may experience the complete set of emotions a surprise elicits when she falls in love with the object and purchases it, knowing many others have passed by this "gem." A find in plain sight for us was a blanket chest, displayed for all to see in a dealer's booth at a show during antiques week in Manchester, that we purchased days later (pictured in *Come Collect with Me*).

Finds are no stranger in our house and one of my favorites spoke to me on a trip, my first to England and my first time in Harrods. This was long before the Internet so a Harrod's teddy bear was a must purchase as was tea to bring home. I did not even know that the famed firm had a Silver Room (which I believe no longer exists). I was not looking to purchase a piece of silver or for anything special. But for whatever reason this teapot spoke to me. It represents one of the highlights of the trip and brings back positive memories each time I look at it. As someone who drinks tea but not coffee (if you ever had tasted my mother's coffee you would know why) the teapot, which I use from time to time, was an unexpected find.

We owned no pieces of antique silver until its purchase, had not really thought of owning any. Yet for whatever reason this English (see the previous chapter on collectors' freedom to put together a collection however they like) made me smile. It made me giddy when I first saw it and resonated with me. It was in its own way hiding in plain sight. Since its purchase we have fallen in love with coin silver spoons and display quite a few. And just as the book went to press, I purchased my first American silver teapot at auction.

I know from my own collecting experience that one thrill of the hunt is unexpectantly spotting something wonderful, a piece you can capture for your collection. I have been to numerous shows and left empty handed. Some shows I return to on their second day, knowing that dealers add new items to their booths. To discover an antique to treasure on the second day of a show, with the crowds much lessened, the aisles much emptier, is somehow more exciting than seeing it during the show's opening. To discover a piece that I love so very much, the silver teapot in a department store, perhaps *the* department store, was a treat. Living with it is even more enjoyable.

Sometimes nice antiques really do sit in chicken coops and in barns. The Hoadley and Thomas wooden works tall case clock (pictured in *Come Collect with Me*) in our collection, complete with mouse hole (now repaired), truly was found in a chicken coop in New Hampshire by a very well-known picker. Cleaned up and with other slight repairs, it is a wonderful piece of painted Americana.

Finds demand that the psychology of surprise—a feeling of astonishment, wonder, and amazement—be explored. Surprise brings the unexpected into collectors' daily routines and lives. It carries with it vitality. Any collector who has unearthed a "find" knows the feeling of freezing in his tracks (for 1/25th of a second the research reports), his attention riveted on the antique he has unexpectedly discovered. Cares and worries, the humdrum of his life disappear for here is something that must be attended to. His entire focus shifts. He may ask himself, "How did this happen? How lucky am I? Where did the dealer find it? Oh, how I hope I can afford it." And surprises make great stories.

In other words, surprises (finds) lessen the stagnation and routine a collector may be feeling and have fallen into. For surprises intensify collectors' feelings—hearts beating faster, breaths taken away. Collectors know that this is an important moment. The collector has discovered something precious, a wonderful antique for his collection, one he did not expect to encounter, which makes its discovery so much more pleasurable.

I hate to suggest that anything about collecting is or becomes routine, but anyone who has sat and reviewed half-a-dozen auction catalogues the same day must—unless inhuman—sigh as he says, "Oh, another Paul Revere spoon." The gift given by surprise is that is breaks a collector's mind away from enforced routine and makes it suddenly comprehend originality, the unexpected, and the unappreciated.

Think about it. If a collector attends an antique show and knows the dealers who have pieces that fit into his collection, he may expect to bring one home. While he may be pleased and smile as he places the cup in a cupboard or on a shelf, hangs the drawing on a wall, or stands the piece of stoneware on the floor, the feeling simply does not compare to making a "find." The unexpected is simply delicious. Yes, old time dealers, bless them, orchestrated surprises, hiding away great antiques in the corners of their shops. A collector had to work to discover them. Do dealers still do that today, i.e., choreograph finds? If not, I wish they did, although I know of a few who think of placing items on their websites in the wee hours of the morning as doing just that.

Surprises bring pleasure. If you doubt me compare your feelings about flowers or chocolates someone unexpectantly gave you with the flowers or sweets, you purchased for yourself. Finds are the spice of a collector's life.

A find can be a form or example a collector did not know existed. My wife is a fan of the Women Airforce Service Pilots (WASPs), women who flew during World War II. Imagine her surprise when she saw a poster at an online auction for the Betsy Ross Corps, a forerunner of the WASPs that existed for only a few years (1931-1933). Not only did she never know of this organization but neither did the curator at the WASP World War II Museum in Texas and Sandy gifted the poster (which she successfully won at auction) to it. How exciting and what a story!

The knowledge of possession also must be considered. "I have it!" Consider the collector who at two in the morning checked a dealer's website and purchased an antique just posted for viewing. "It is mine and mine alone." This elicited feeling of possession is powerful. With the feeling of possession comes a feeling of specialness. "I was the only collector smart enough to rummage in the very back of the cupboard and look what it got me." Or "My preparation and study paid off when I saw beyond the dust and hodgepodge in the dealer's shop to bring forth this wonderful small painting."

I am not singing the praises of selfishness here but the

sense of having one's efforts and study meet with success brings a smile to a collector. Setting aside the element of luck (see Chapter 14), it is not too long a stretch to say finds are the product of refined knowledge and hard work. Over time, the prepared collector accumulates a catalogue of desirables and their characteristics. When the moment arrives (it may never do so, of course) the axons sputter, the eyes widen, the heartbeat rises, and the Discovery becomes the Possession.

A dealer was prowling an "antique mall, mostly collectibles to tell the truth." He found a china plate that he purchased for a dollar and sold for $100. Not truly a wonderful find, except the plate represented his greatest return on investment to this day (he sold it for 100 times what he paid). Or the collector prowling a group shop finds a rare piece of signed American metalware, 17th century, only one of a few known. A bona fide find to say the least. Collecting does not get any better than continuously seeking a truly rare piece and finally unexpectantly finding one.

One could argue that even the Amni Phillips, *Woman with Pink Ribbons* (1833) that sold for $3,870,000 at the January 2022 Christie's auction in New York City was a find if the collectors who purchased it were looking for a crown jewel in their collection, money was no object and fell in love with the painting. I believe the latter (falling in love) is the key to the painting being a find (in plain sight). American antiques in seven figures do come along now and then, but loving one is another matter. Christies described the painting as

Vibrant, minimalist and mesmerizingly beautiful, this portrait of a Woman with Pink Ribbons stands as one of Ammi Phillips' masterpieces. Here, Phillips has brought the sitter forward and only included the smallest of background details, resulting in a powerful composition with maximum impact. The neckline of the sitter's dress and the flanking billowing sleeves, the wide waistband, hint of the sofa rail and position of the left arm all work together to emphasize the horizontal axis, while the movement of the ribbons echoed in the shimmer of the dress create a sense of circular movement within the central field. The sitter's plain dress and fashionable large sleeves also allowed the artist to render planes of unfettered color. These expanses of green with contrasting pink highlights have been likened by Stacy C. Hollander, former Chief Curator and Deputy Director of the American Folk Art Museum, to the masterful tableaus of Mark Rothko.

I have been told by several who have seen the painting in person that it has great presence and is quite beautiful.

Ordinary things for other people—spoons, clothing, books —can be wonders to someone who truly knows what they signify—survival though the ages, extraordinary craftsmanship, a mind revealed. What we call finds are not somethings that come into existence all of a sudden, but things that come into our existence. They were never part of our lives and suddenly they are. The differences between the mundane and the wonderful come from two things: our knowledge and our feelings. Approach the potential find as someone ignorant and it looks ordinary. Approach it as someone who does not care, and it looks worthless. But see it as informed eyes and an open heart and we are breathless ... "What a find!"

From a one-dollar plate to Amni Phillip's painting, finds come from all sorts of venues, in all sorts of genres with varying price points. One of the joys of collecting is the surprise of a find. However, defined, and wherever collectors discover a "find," the feelings they experience, and the memories of the event are a major part of the joys and excitement of collection. William S. Burroughs (American writer and visual artist, and a voice of the beat generation) may have writing about collecting when he wrote that "life is surprise." Collectors know how right he is. Our silver teapot is testimony to Burroughs' observation.

CHAPTER 21

Pitfalls in Making Good Decisions as a Collector

Experienced collectors have learned a thing or two, especially when it comes to deciding which pieces to add to their collections. They know that forces weigh on them, sometimes only on the edges of awareness or hidden altogether, and not always positive. Nor is the collector's thinking always "rational." Let's look at some of the traps and dynamics of collecting. As the proverb says, "To be forewarned is to be forearmed."

Confirmation bias is a way of approaching decisions in which individuals tend to interpret information in a manner that confirms their present beliefs or values. A collector interprets new information, or rejects it, to bring it in line with what he has already surmised. *Self-verification theory* is similar. People prefer feedback from others that is consistent with their own self and worldviews.

Duncan really liked a piece of silver at auction. A dealer looked at it for him and reported condition problems not listed in the auction house description and added that he thought the estimate was high. Not what Duncan wanted to hear. A friend told him the piece was "nice," just what he wanted to hear. Duncan discounted the dealer's information and exceeded his decided upon upper limit, paying a pretty penny. Moral: Keep your wits about you and listen carefully.

Yielding to a group's consensus—*conformity*—can trip up even the most experienced collector. Group or individual's pressure can be a powerful persuader.

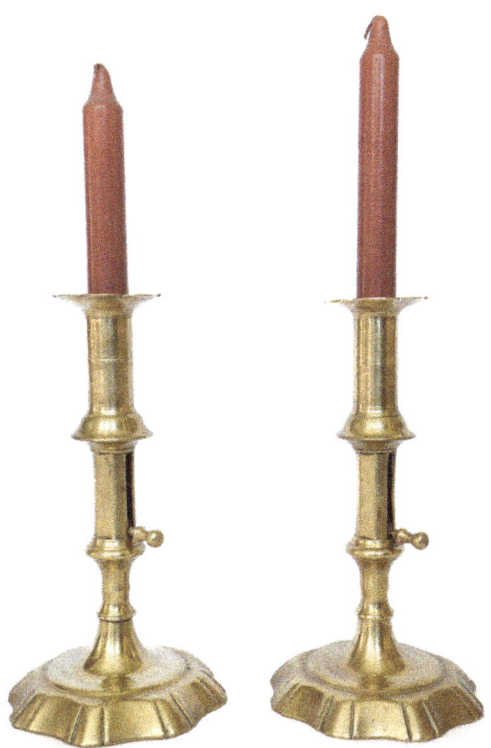

Kenneth kept in close touch with a group of collectors who prized condition, provenance, and form. He shared his interest in adding another set of candlesticks to his collection. To a person, each one he asked disapproved of the two pairs he had his eyes on. Kenneth gave up the idea, knuckling under to the group's views. As time passed his decision niggled at him. Eventually he broke free of conforming to the group's wishes and bought a pair of sticks he very much enjoyed. Moral: Others' feedback can be valuable, but not always. After all, it is your collection.

We once had a dealer tell us that any good collection needed a lowboy. We chose to ignore his advice, and our collection does not conform to his beliefs. The space where it would have gone in our home is filled with a painted Federal card table that we like very much.

We have had people tell us that they do not like the fact that the candlesticks pictured are pushups. They like earlier sticks. Perhaps we would consider a pair of 17th century Dutch candlesticks? We have a pair of earlier English sticks but wanted a different look. In the 18th century a change in design and manufacturing allowed for production of slide ejectors with a handle on the side. A collector will also find candlesticks with push-rod ejectors underneath the base. This change allowed for ease in pushing the remands of the candle up the stick's stem so it could be easily removed.

We ignored the advice for earlier sticks because we like these candlesticks and the history in manufacturing that they represent. They are an example that a collection reflects the personal taste of the collectors who have put it together. In our case that means candlesticks such as these, and we own a second pair of pushups with a different style base.

Groupthink (the term was coined in 1952) occurs when

a group of individuals reaches a consensus with the goal of harmony or conformity. A classic example of groupthink is the failure of the space shuttle Challenger wherein engineers gave approval to the launch. Desire to maintain the cohesiveness of the group (consciously or unconsciously) led to agreement and independent decision making was run roughshod by the group's *esprit de corps*.

A well-known auction house obtained a prestigious collection. But when its senior Americana specialist, Donald, looked closely many pieces had flaws. Donald shared his findings with other staff, but everyone kept quiet, and the flaws went unmentioned. No one wanted to toss a pebble in the water and watch the ripples spread. Moral: Team morale and togetherness are fine until they aren't.

The *Present Bias* reflects the tendency to prize immediate rewards over long-term goals.

Edgar saw a piece of painted tinware in a form he liked, in average condition, and purchased it. However, better pieces became available and at better prices as well. His thinking, "I want something now" was ill advised. In time Edgar, a relatively new collector, learned to wait and delay immediate gratification, a sign of maturity in a collector. Moral: The inner urge to buy can be powerful. Fight it with all you have.

Another trap for collectors is called *Base Rate Neglect* (part of the *Availability Heuristic*) and reflects the tendency to judge the probability of something happening based on easily accessible information (that may be incorrect or simplistic) while ignoring important data or subtleties. The availability heuristic can be defeated by careful study. Collectors then learn what is available and are not hostage to the more common varieties they see time and time again.

Malcolm received both *Maine Antique Digest* and *Antiques and the Arts Weekly* (*The Bee*) on the same day. Prices seemed to be rising for the small painted boxes he loved. Overreacting to this information and not paying attention to these boxes' condition, Malcolm quickly purchased two he later regretted owning. His mistake: He ignored other resources of information and overgeneralized from the articles he had read to the entire market. With due diligence he would have learned that only the best of the best was rising substantially in price. His easily gotten information led him stray. Moral: Do your homework and know the market. Knowledge is power for the collector.

Every collector should be aware of being *overconfident*.

Henry prided himself on his eye, and his ability to quickly discern if a piece was right. While attending a high-end show he saw a Windsor braceback chair he liked. Briefly looking at it he told the dealer he would take it. Only when he brought the Windsor home did he give it a thorough inspection and was dismayed with its condition. Henry's overconfidence proved his Windsor downfall. Moral: Beware of considering yourself the smartest person in the room.

Loss Aversion should be understood by collectors. People feel greater emotions for loss than they do for gains. None the less, collectors are sometimes smarter to accept losing money on some pieces as simply part of "the game." Taking a loss does not reflect poorly on collectors Instead, it reflects a knowledge of the market and the desire to continue to build a collection.

Henry did not know what to do with his Windsor chair. He kicked himself for having purchased it. He had learned a valuable lesson, that he should take more time to look at pieces when at a show. Although selling the chair would mean a loss in dollars, he overcame his feelings of loss aversion. The chair was put up for auction and sold. Moral: Learn to lose and from your mistakes and move on.

Cognitive Dissonance occurs when a person's behaviors are inconsistent with his values or self-image. What results is an uncomfortable, often anxiety-ridden, stressful feeling people attempt to undo it by their actions.

While at a show that featured textiles James encountered a dealer that he had bought from some time ago. The dealer was honest, had nice goods for sale, and she had even contacted him once or twice over the years He had never responded. James felt he had treated her badly and purchased a men's waistcoat from her, more to salve his own conscience and make amends than anything else. He owned better examples. But he felt better upon leaving her booth. A simple conversation with her and perhaps an apology might have saved him money and accomplished the same end. Moral: Examine your motivations, feelings of anxiety and unsettledness carefully.

In-group bias involves benefiting someone in your group, as opposed to someone outside your group.

Over time, Robert had developed a relationship with

a group of dealers he considered his go-to folks when he wanted to add to his collection. He never considered enlarging the group to include two or three up-and-coming, knowledgeable, younger dealers. His dollars were spent with the dealers in his group but in the long run his collection might have been better had he moved beyond them to others. Moral: Loyalty and a tried-and-true pattern are fine, until they aren't.

Collectors use *baseline comparisons* all the time to decide whether a piece is worth pursuing. Groups influence these baselines by the parameters they set for what is an exceptional, average, or subpar antique.

Mary had found a tallcase clock she liked. Reaching out to fellow collectors for their opinions, they pointed out its flaws (in their eyes). The dealer told her that for the price the clock was fine. Mary ended up not purchasing it. The collectors to whom she listened were using criteria closer to a museum-grade piece, not a clock that was solid, affordable, and would have brought her much enjoyment. Moral: Make sure the baseline others use for what is a good antique matches your own.

"Good decisions come from experience and experience comes from making poor decisions." (anonymous) No collector is immune from "irrational" thoughts and others' opinions. The world of Americana is as messy a universe as any that collectors encounter—work, family, marriages, finances, and the like. If you have recently made a good decision as a collector sleep well tonight. And if you have made a poor decision but learned from it, sleep even better. (And thanks to the rulers of Scotland for the examples in this chapter.)

CHAPTER 22

Quitting

In recent years several behavioral traits have been lauded as keys to success—persistence, grit, and determination, to name a few. Less well known is the value of quitting. After all, successful card players quit much more than they stay in the game. Kenny Rogers said it best: "You've got to know when to hold 'em. Know when to fold 'em. Know when to walk away. And know when to run." Note that three of the four options require quitting.

The problem with extolling the value of quitting is that it has a bad rap. You are not a coward if you quit, despite all the oaters (old westerns) you may have watched growing up. What is true grit worth if you stick with things that are no longer worthwhile? Are you determined to be a good singer or dancer but are terrible at both (as am I)? A bit foolish, isn't it? I know that being called a "quitter" stings but there are tines collectors should wear the label with pride. The trick is to pick the right things to keep doing, in the right situation—knowing when to "hold 'em"—and at the same time, be prepared to "fold 'em" when they are or turn bad. Using that knowledge is a lifelong task whether the venue is a disagreement with a spouse, a business decision or collecting.

In our society we do not like the word "quit." We talk

instead of "pivoting" or "taking a sabbatical" or "moving on the next chapter of our lives"—all wonderful euphemisms for packing it in. Yet such decisions can reflect great wisdom. The scientific research supports the idea that we often persevere too long, often in the face of bad news. Sometimes we over-sustain and then wonder why things did not work out, wearing ourselves out in the process.

A collector highly covets a piece up for auction. As the bidding climbs, he reassesses both his love for the object and his bank account, finally deciding to fold his tent. In the heat of the moment, and with love for an object urging him on, said collector may be hard put to quit. It is the reason some collectors leave a bid or have a dealer bid for them, avoiding the venue altogether. It makes it easier to say "no", for the most difficult time to make a quitting decision is when you are in the moment.

Collectors also can be outpriced for an item in a private sale, at a dealer's shop or in a show booth. Despite interest and love, if the price is too high, and no financial machinations bring it within reach, a wise collector quits. Quitting in such a situation often feels like quitting too soon. "There must be a way to finance the purchase," the collector tells himself. "I need to think about it longer." "I need to be more creative." My advice: "Fold 'em."

Of course, quitting makes a collector invisible, at least for the moment. She did not pay a record-setting price for the antique at the auction with the attendant publicity. But being invisible is okay if a collector lives (at least financially) to collect another day.

Such decision-making can be tricky. Collectors often do not have all the facts, though that dos does not absolve them from doing their research. They do not know how luck will play a part (or not) in their present and future collecting. At the very moment they are deciding or even afterwards, new information sometimes becomes available. Regret or relief may be the result. It therefore behooves collectors to find advice-givers and role models for quitting. Collectors need friends and dealers who understand their financial situation, for example, who can advise them to pull the plug, to give it up, to quit. "You simply cannot afford this antique" may be the best advice a collector has heard. Knowing you can quit makes collecting easier, not more difficult.

I am at a first-rate and much-anticipated show. I have walked the floor and walked it again. Objects are beginning to blur; I am tired. Yet pieces in booths are displayed I have not closely examined. What to do? Quit. Leave the venue and get out into the fresh air. Go to lunch and talk about anything but antiques. Sit and gather myself. But I hear you saying, "There may be an antique he really would have wanted that sold while he was taking a time out." True enough. But I probably would not have seen or appreciated it anyway. I was spent (as my kids used to say, he was fizzed). I can return to the show reinvigorated with a better chance of making good decisions. An antique missed—possibly. But that is always true. Collectors must learn to live with uncertainty.

In this instance I did not follow my own advice. This small circa 1900 lipstick red pantry box sits in our stack of painted boxes. It should not be resting there. I purchased it at a show when I was tired. I was looking for a small box, and I liked the form. But there were better boxes available in dealers' shops (pictured online), earlier, some with a "finger" or two, some with a "softer" color, blue or yellow, or a faded pale green, and some wear. Had I taken a break I would have passed on this box and found one that made me smile. The cost was not insurmountable, so the lesson I learned was not too dear. Still, I should have known better. I can always find another box and put it under this one or just above it.

Collectors and the genres they collect often involves quitting. Some collectors, let us say of painted furniture, if circumstances allow, will come to purchase more expensive pieces than they presently own. Those that used to give them so much pleasure no longer do so. Some finally "get rid of" a piece they have not liked since the day they purchased it. Some move on to different genres. Some decide they can live with imperfections and stop sending pieces to the best of restorers. Some quit collecting American antiques but continue to collect something else. Some quit collecting all together. You can call these decisions growth, life changing, or simply deciding what will make a particular collector happy. New or different genres or leaving collecting can be risky, for there is no guarantee the decision will bring the pleasure and satisfaction that the collector anticipates.

Collectors and genres impart an important lesson—quitting is not always about money. It often is about things much more important—meaning, enjoyment, or new opportunities to name but three. If what a collector is doing now, in what she collects, who she works with, what she is spending, makes her unhappy or feels simply blah, and she anticipates it will continue to do so, what does she have to lose by quitting? Nothing. Research shows that once people leave something (e.g., a job, a marriage) that feels like a "close call" (many positives on both sides of the decision) quitters often are happier than those who stick it out.

Collectors need be aware of what is called "escalation of commitment." People tend to over-persist despite data that they should do the opposite, that is, walk away. Part of the reason is that we believe that the money, time, even commitment we have put in a poker pot is still ours—"sunk costs" they are called. If I research a piece for hours and hours, talk with my favorite dealer about it, travel to the auction where it will be put up for bid, have time, money, and fantasies of owning it all expended, it may be difficult for me to assess my bids realistically and walk away.

Successful collectors of American antiques must take the view that collecting is a long-term endeavor. One piece, one show, one auction, does not make a good collection. To be successful collectors simply need to win more than they lose over time. Does knowing all this affect the doing of collecting? The research shows it does not. An intellectual understanding, an education in why it is so difficult to pivot and quit, does not make the quitting any easier.

What makes quitting so difficult is that collectors are doing more than pivoting away from genres they collect, shows they attend, or dealers they purchase from. They are altering their identities by focusing on something different. "I am no longer a collector of great painted furniture," or "I do not attend the wonderful shows the way I used to; age has crept up on me." Sometimes it is not the world that changes, but we who do so. Our likes do not always remain static for a lifetime. Losing or changing part of our collector identities can be painful and is a primary determinant of maintaining the status quo.

That stable world we all want is powerful (the "status quo bias" it is called) and finding different collecting paths can be arduous and burdensome, despite the acknowledged need to do so. Collectors often like things, for the most part, the way they are. Errors of commission are visible to them but errors of omission (I should have collected something different years ago) are camouflaged and often beyond collectors' awareness except in retrospect. Better the devil you know. But there comes a time to move on. Not everything is forever. Once a collector knows that the "expected value" of doing things the way he always has is too high, it is time to change.

It might be valuable if an antique show now and then, had "round tables", each with a different topic (like some professional conventions) where collectors could discuss and hash out issues of collecting, including quitting. I'd be happy to arrange such a venue, if asked. That way someone might become a "quitting coach," helping collectors to see valuable fresh perspectives.

Have I convinced you to become aware of both your status quo and quitting behaviors? I hope so. Such awareness is a good tool for a collector to have. So, at that auction, "hold 'em," certainly. But "fold 'em," walk or run away on occasion. You'll be a better collector for doing so.

CHAPTER 23

A World Gone By

"... carry this, [a plastic bucket] and you carry the chemicals and factories of this century." He [a lama] lifted a wooden pail and said, "Carry this and you are the novice taking water to the first lamas of Tibet or the boy watering the yaks of a salt caravan four hundred years ago."

Soul of the Fire, Pattison

Why do collectors purchase objects crafted decades or centuries ago? What are they preserving? In rereading copies of *Maine Antique Digest*, I had a wonderful opportunity and a front row seat to material culture that has passed into history, or at least is on its way. From objects for the poor to those for the wealthy, a way of life that once was vibrant and taken for granted has disappeared. Collectors of Americana clutch that history in the pieces they pursue, purchase, and display. In essence collecting American antiques helps keep bygone eras alive.

What objects will be collected and whose purpose will cause people to scratch their heads in bewilderment in the years ahead—mimeograph machines, overhead projectors, landline telephones (although I still have one at home), automobiles with crank handles that lower windows, electric typewriters, hand calculators that cost hundreds of dollars when new? There is already talk of vintage Ikea furniture. (I wonder if it is worth more if still in the box?)

Let us begin with closets, or their absence to be more accurate. Closets in homes did not become more common until the early to mid-1800s. Until then clothing, linens, and other objects were stored in Kas, Schranks, and blanket cases or chests, to name but a few. The 1820s Federal-style home of John Quincy Adams has a closet, measuring only 2 feet by 4 feet. What collectors of Americana are preserving by collecting free standing pieces of furniture is testimony to the long-past absence of a recessed space with a door.

Gentility is also being preserved, a certain refinement and genteel customs that have disappeared. Not merely for the wealthy but let us begin with them. I read (not in *MAD*) of a set of silver with a place setting for 80! Not only the size of this set of silver struck me. It was housed in a specially built chest with five drawers. The specialized pieces of silver boggle the mind—tongs for asparagus, tongs for sugar (cut from solid pieces and then locked away), spoons for this and that, silver salts, and the unimaginable. Also in use were coffee and tea services (also sometimes in pewter). I immediately thought of *Downton Abbey*.

My wife and I have a set of China that was my grand-mother's. We should use it but for some reason we do not. It would go well with a set of silver that also was hers. Why we use our "everyday" dishes and cutlery is beyond me. Perhaps it is habit, or we have lost a sense of refinement that would enrich our lives. I feel decadent when I use our antique silver teapot. I like the almost shameless feeling it elicits. The set of dishes and the silver cutlery would increase our daily sense of decorousness and poshness that seems in short supply in our society.

Where would the china and silver be stored? Those of us who collect Americana preserve the dining room. Dining rooms are disappearing in new houses I am told. Are they making a comeback? Any antique dealer is ecstatic to sell a sideboard nowadays and ones crafted in the South fetch goodly sums.

We preserve security. In the dining room one might also find valuables, such as sugar, so valuable that sugar chests had locks as did tea caddies. The lady or mistress of the house had the keys so the contents could be kept safe. By 1750, sugar had surpassed grain as the "most valuable commodity in European trade. It was an expensive commodity, known as "white gold." To cut the sugar one used sugar nippers. Tea became more affordable by the middle 1700s when the East India Company increased its supply.

Other valuables, such as documents were often kept in drop-front desks with locks, or even hidden compartments. Linens and other household items must also have been valuable as blanket chests often had locks as well.

Americana collectors also conserve a world of dried food-stuffs before plastic containers were ubiquitous. The variety of wooden containers boggles the mind—keelers, firkins, pantry boxes oval and round, salt boxes, tureen cannisters. Do an experiment. Look in a pantry or the herb and spice shelf or two in a cupboard and take each of the herbs out of its plastic or glass container. The herbs must be stored somewhere, the parsley, sage, rosemary, and thyme (thank you Simon and Garfunkel), allspice, basil, chive, mint, marjoram, savory, oregano, licorice, yarrow, ginger, clove, horsetail, and more. Grown in gardens, the herbs were probably fresher than many we purchase today.

Collectors also preserve the bride's wedding day, treasuring highly decorated wooden bride boxes. In an article in *Early American Life* (June 2012) the author tells us they were often gifts and used for trinkets, mementos, small items, and keepsakes, the equivalent of 18th-century wedding photos. They regularly appear in the marketplace.

One sees a great many cutlery carriers on the market. It seems they were in wide use in the 19th century. Staying in the kitchen whether as part of the house or a separate building bird spits and spit engines, and other fireplace accoutrements are collected and still used. How wonderful that a basic foodstuff like butter was made fancy with wonderful butter prints. And where to put delicious pies and keep them safe— pie safes of course.

Collectors preserve a world before Tupperware and refrigerators. Stoneware and woodenware were used to store and preserve a variety of edibles—potatoes, yams, carrots, and other necessities from the garden as well as meat (mainly beef, pork and mutton) along with animal fats, including lard and butter.

Americana collectors also celebrate walls. With floor space and cupboards often in short supply walls were used in ways that have disappeared. A variety of wall boxes and pipe boxes were in use, as were salt boxes, small hanging cupboards, spoon racks, string dispensers, and a variety of mirrors (they could not be hung on the back of closet doors -- no closets, remember?).

Collectors remember the act and art of play before video games, cell phones and the Internet. Americana has its game boards, a mark that some leisure time existed for checkers, chess, parchisi, and others. Game tables brought enjoyment, many to be folded and put against a wall when not in use. Often the checker/chess board was inlaid, and fancy game tables had felt tops with rounded corners where candlesticks were placed for a game of whist.

Then there are toys. Toys to be handled and played with, hoops and dolls. Some toys made of tin or heavier metal, colorful in nature. Trains, planes autos, boats, horse drawn carriages, trolleys. Some could be wound up or had mechanisms to allow moving parts. Märklin made wonderful clockwork ships. Mechanical banks were popular in all sorts of forms. A Merry Go Round or Red Riding Hood bank for example, turn the clank and the penny disappears. I wonder if children today would know how to play with such a toy, desire one, cherish one like in the days of yore.

Homes had to have light once the sun set, whether with basic rush holders or fancy chandeliers with candles galore. Lanterns, slide boxes to hold candles, candlesticks, whale oil lamps, and kerosene lamps (more recent). When the power goes out, lighting them changes our home's ambiance for the better.

A simple rush light sits on a Queen Anne table in our living room and has done so for decades. We have never used it. To do so we would strip most of the tough outer fiber of the stem of a rush, exposing the pith. We would then dip what remains of the rush in melted fat, light it, and use it as a taper for illumination. The rushlight would be dipped once or only a few times and is too soft and thin to stand in a candlestick. At one point in time, we had a piece of rush in the holder, but our cats made quick work of it. The rush light reminds us of how basic lighting was important and special centuries ago.

Of course, collectors fill their homes with American antique furniture, large and small. The need for candles for most people has passed but candlestands make excellent tables next to a wingback chair on which to put a fine glass of wine or scotch as one reads on a winter day. Lowboys and highboys are bygone chests of drawers. Dropfront desks have suffered in popularity because one cannot easily put a desktop computer on one and close the lid, although laptops work fine. Cupboards of all shapes and sizes—built in, chimney, etc. Does anyone build a home today or remodel a condo with built in cupboards? Tables of all varieties from drop leaf to harvest, Pembroke, or those used in a kitchen. Tables are still bought and manufactured today but buy an antique one if you want quality.

Tea tables abound and while high tea and the drinking of tea has experienced a resurgence how many folks purchase a table simply on which to set the accouterments? Tavern tables make wonderful, useful tables for all sorts of purposes. Will there be a Starbucks or an Applebee's table someday? Tables were often pushed to the wall, so they had legs that swung out and tops that unfolded. Shoe foot trestle tables also served more than one need. With their folding tops they also could be pushed to a wall after tea, a meal, or a game of checkers.

I have not broached the subject of the toilette—washstands, potty chairs, and bowls and pitchers. Or how people used to dress. And a world before cameras, replete with portrait paintings, silhouettes, limns of schooners and other ships, one's prize animal or farm. The telling of time became more important and thus watch hutches for pocket watches and an array of tallcase and shelf clocks. Rope beds (sleep tight), no box springs back then. Painted tin, leather fire buckets, key baskets, metal work crafted by blacksmiths —rams head hinges, Indian head hinges. Glass bottles for liquids—bourbon, bitters, half-pint and pint, and quart flasks, and much more recently milk. How we used to advertise!—wooden barber poles, shoe repair signs in the shape of shoes, clock repair and sale signs in the shapes of clock dials. Finally, how we used to make things—no battery powered power tools: planes, brass squares, axes, swages, hand-built tool chests, wrenches, beautiful bit braces.

Whether with a single object, a room of American antiques, or an entire house, collectors, for the moment, in their imagination, leave this world behind. And they will tell you they are better for having done so.

A Māori proverb reads: "I walk backwards into the future with my eyes fixed on my past." Substitute the word "the" for "my" and many collectors of American antiques will tell you that is one of their most important goals—preserving, reveling in, and making sure the past is not forgotten. I am sure I have only touched on this preservation.

CHAPTER 24

Displaying Antiques
to Their Best Advantage

Many collectors live day-to-day with their collections. Whether arrayed throughout their homes, barns, or offices, or displayed on shelves in a "special" room devoted to that purpose, the antiques typically are in full view. But how does one arrange them to their best advantage? How best to present the antiques so they garner the admiring glances and touches they fully deserve? The goal: "A home should feel collected, not decorated." (Albert Hadley, designer, and decorator) At the same time some collectors want their homes to feel like a museum of colonial times; others opt for practicality.

Think of a collector of train sets. Typically shelves or cases hold their prized transportation toys, often with appropriate lighting so that details shall not be missed. The possibilities of how to arrange these trains are nearly endless. The collector can display them by manufacturer, size, color, age, or mix and match to his own preferences. Rare pieces can be in one spot, perhaps fewer of them so each train locomotive or car is highlighted.

When it comes to displaying American antiques and creating an aesthetically pleasing arrangement, several rules of thumb exist that can guide collectors to showcase their collections to their best advantage, while at the same time being comfortable to live with. A collector can have great fun taking one room in his house and rearranging antiques according to one of the "rules" below or realizing he already has done so, putting into words the why's and what's of the arrangement(s).

Less is More

My wife has said this decorating law to me so many times it is deeply ingrained in my psyche. My problem as a collector is that as I add to our collection it is becoming difficult to obey. A collector is advised to avoid cluttering the space with too many items. One way to do this is to continually upgrade a collection so that the antiques one owns are "good ones", selling lesser pieces. Or at least displaying only part of a collection and putting the rest away, rotating the pieces perhaps. Collectors must realize that merely because they have purchased a painting, piece of redware or furniture they do not have to live with it forever. Rather than an attic or basement, consign it to an auction house, give it to a child or friend (if they will have it and depending on its financial worth).

Butting heads with less is more are the pieces the collector wants to display because of emotional attachment or the wonderful stories that accompany them. A tale of discovery ought to be in full view. And all collectors have their indispensable favorites. These antiques form the core with other pieces orbiting around them.

Less is more does not mean that many smalls cannot be grouped. A stepback or other type of cupboard is a wonderful vehicle for displaying a collection of redware or other smalls. But a collector would not want several such cupboards and displays in his home, at least not contiguous or in the same room. Just as at an antique show one piece, by itself, can really stand out. Displaying a collection according to this maxim forces the collector to decide what the key pieces are. Then each can be appreciated individually. The visual display is often enhancing and balanced.

Group Similar Items When Appropriate

Typically, these items are smalls although collectors of stoneware often have a dozen or more on the floor together or on an, often expensive bucket bench. But Sandy and I would not think of putting our firkins together as they would lose their pop. A collector can group items based on their theme (the Connecticut room, the Queen Anne period). Perhaps all painted pieces of various genre are displayed together. In our corner cupboard some of our redware collection is displayed, the rest in a cupboard in the dining room. Grouping similar pieces creates what is thought of as a "cohesive display" and highlights differences between the pieces. For example, a collector could group antique silver or painted tin boxes.

Vary Heights and Sizes

Visual interest is enhanced by incorporating items of different heights and sizes. This adds "dimension" to the display and presents it from looking flat. Common sense rules: Taller items should be displayed behind smaller and shorter ones. Following this maxim is typically easily accomplished. Paintings, painted boxes, redware, silver, and the like typically vary in heights and sizes.

Weathervanes stood on cupolas or roofs on the top of barns, churches and homes. They were meant to be seen from below. We have purposely put this horse and sulky weathervane (that we recently upgraded to) as high as we could get it in the room and home. People who have seen it tell us it looks wonderful on top of the corner cupboard in the living room. Some especially like the tableau of the vane and the shadow it sometimes casts, depending on the time of day and year, on the wall behind it. An eagle weathervane we own sits atop a highboy, again as high as we could find a place for it (pictured in Chapter 30).

Pay Attention to Proportion

Consider the size of the antiques and the scale of the space and then move forward. Large pieces can overpower a small room. The obverse also is true: Tiny objects may become lost in a larger space. Proportion is one reason my wife and I do not own any "large" paintings. Our home is modest, and we simply lack the room and wall size to display a large painting properly.

Color Harmony

I will now move onto more shaky ground, considering I

am not an accomplished "decorator." Some collectors attend to "color harmony." They consider the colors of the antiques in their home and how the pieces will interact with the existing color scheme of the room. They may even harmonize the colors by grouping similar tones together or by using complementary colors to create a focal point. Phew! My wife and I do none of these things. We believe our oriental rugs and antiques are works of art and place them irrespective of their colors. No doubt we will be damned for doing so but we find our home peaceful to live in and love the way it looks.

Balance and Symmetry

On the other hand, we do attend to balance and symmetry. Balance is achieved by distributing the visual "weight" of a collection evenly. For instance, we have a cupboard in the kitchen that takes up some space. It is balanced with a hanging shelf with small items on the oppositive wall. Symmetry can create a sense of order, even elegance. At the least a room does not feel like it is tilted.

Mindful Placement

This principle is an important one, taking some awareness and trial and error. Mindful placemen suggests that a collector pay attention to the placement of his antiques, the flow of the room and the natural path the eye follows. Collectors are urged to place the most captivating or significant items at eye level or in prominent locations to draw attention.

I admit my wife and I have struggled with mindful place-ment. Yes, some special antiques are fully visible. On the other hand, our corner cupboard in the living room has an upper door with glass (as one might expect). But a couple wonderful redware pieces, put on shelves therein, are difficult to see. We are loathe to put them on tabletops with "brackets' to support them, having Roscoe and Quimby (our cats) as family members. And we lack the wall space to display them there. Some silver is displayed in a built-in dining room cupboard, where again, the pieces are difficult to see. I can only conclude that mindful placement is an aspirational goal, never fully realized.

Lighting Matters

It is not unusual for a collector attending a show to ask a dealer if an item can be taken outside the venue to see it in natural light. Oftentimes the pieces come alive in this setting. Proper lighting can significantly enhance the display of a collector's antiques. I do not know if my wife and I are unusual, but we do not have accent lighting in our home to highlight key pieces, thus losing an opportunity to create drama and add warmth. Lamps are situated primarily for reading; overhead lighting is limited or absent. We succeed in having no harsh or direct lighting that may damage more delicate items (e.g., quilts, millinery pieces). We have no lighting over our paintings although I am considering adding it to one or two.

Thoughtful Backdrops

Collectors are urged to choose appropriate backdrops that enhance the beauty and character of their antiques. They are advised to consider solid-colored walls, neutral fabrics (drapes, etc.) or textured wallpapers that can provide a suitable surface that allows the focus to remain on the antiques. While our home is not colonial in its exterior style, we succeed in meeting this maxim by having white walls in all our rooms with painted woodwork (of different colors) in each. The walls allow for a good display of paintings, clocks, brushes (we have a grouping of shaker and other brushes in the kitchen). The painted woodwork in each room is ignored. The only tension in all this is our stairway to the upstairs. The walls, congruent with their height and size, are covered with a (large) patterned wallpaper. I would love to hang paintings on these walls, expanding our collection. My wife says the wallpaper is not a thoughtful backdrop. We agree to disagree, and the walls are unadorned.

Consider a Surprise

A special antique that is jarring in its display will certainly be noticed and stand out. Toss out most of what you have read above and put a piece from a different era, material, location, or size amid a thoughtful display. Pow!

Tell a Story

If I lived in a larger home with more wall space, I might have one wall with nothing but nautical paintings and prints. Someone interested in children's lives might have a grouping of a school desk from a one-room school, a reader, and a school clock along with silhouettes and small paintings of youngsters.

Rotate Displays and Even Hide

To avoid habituation to the antiques displayed and to keep the display fresh and interesting, a collector can periodically rotate the items. Put some away and bring them out at a later date. Doing so prevents visual fatigue and allows the collector to showcase different pieces in his collection. Rotating sensitive items such as quilts and other textiles allows a collector to see and enjoy them without placing them at risk. I have tried to do rotate pieces in our collection, and it works, but I do not do it often enough. Perhaps I need to become more intentional to rotating the antiques we own.

Heed Realistic Limitations

Roscoe and Quimby limit our display of very small items that they would simply play with and carry away. Do not hang paintings above radiators. If the children in the home are small, delicate and easily breakable pieces may be put away for the moment, not that teenagers have the best sense of balance and decorum.

It is paramount that I point out that these rules of thumb serve as general guidelines and collectors are free to experiment and trust their likes and intuition. It is the collectors after all who have labored to build a collection and chosen to live with their antiques. Any display will and must reflect the collector's personal style and highlight what she views as the unique and important qualities of the collection. Have fun, be flexible and brave, and tinker to your heart's content.

CHAPTER 25

Four Mysteries in Collecting American Antiques

Mysteries abound in the collecting of American antiques, and I need a detective—Nancy Drew, Rebus, Sherlock Holmes, Harry Bosch, Nora and Nick Charles, or Sam Spade will do just fine. Whether Nero Wolfe tending his orchids in his New York City brownstone (leaving the shoe leather to Archie), or Philip Marlowe in trouble once again with the dames, hopefully these famous gumshoes can shed light on some of the puzzles created by what we collectors do and the antiques we collect.

Three of the mysteries are clearly psychological in origin, and one is based in etymology.

Let us start with a cozy mystery, not a locked-room murder mind you, but interesting just the same. Why do three items make up a collection? Not two mind you, not four or five, but three. I have surveyed the usual suspects, and I am not convinced of their guilt. A collector might haphazardly purchase one or two pieces because of the look, the price, or other reasons. But if he owns three objects of the same genre, I am told that the collector is being intentional.

He certainly could own three of something, I respond and not have a collection. For a collection is not only dependent on the number of pieces, it also is psychological. More than three pairs of shoes grace my closet, but I also do not consider them a collection either.

"Why not four or five?" I inquire. The Beatles have four members, and Dumas' *The Three Musketeers* were not a trio (Aramis, Porthos, Athos, & D'Artagnon). There are Four Horsemen of the Apocalypse (conquest, war, famine & death). "Because that is too many; three it is, because I said so," another collector says, sounding like a three-year-old to me. Three is the magic number—the holy trinity the Magi, the fates of Greek mythology (*Clotho, Lachesis, & Atropos*), the witches in Macbeth, or the number of blind mice.

In other words, three make a collection for the same reason that the television show was called, *Three's Company*. Now that is convincing. Then there is the decorating rule of three: Odd numbers of objects make a more appealing, effective, and memorable display. The same guideline appears in photography, design, and even story telling. It seems that three is the smallest number that we can use to form a distinguishable pattern. It is something that is wired into us at a neurological level.

While our brains feel satisfied with symmetry, adding an odd number of things makes our brain feel challenged and compositions feel more dynamic. Graphic designers and interior decorators use the "rule of three" all the time. Objects grouped into three appear more harmonious. Nike's "Just do it" and McDonald's "I'm lovin' it" slogans are two examples from advertising. In children's literature we have *Goldilocks and the Three Bears* and the fable of *The Three Little Pigs*.

But Sandy and I do have several collections, three or more antiques purchased deliberately. Chapter One contains a photograph of a candlestand. We have several sitting in the house—a collection. In Chapter Two the dial of a wooden works tallcase clock is featured. We have three of such clocks also, another collection. A Windsor rocking chair (tripleback) is presented in Chapter 27. We own three tripleback Windsors, thus another collection. This tome contains three paintings of a view of the Hudson from West Point, and I would like to collect more—a fourth collection. The redware banks in Chapter Nine make up still another collection, as do almost ten pieces of redware with writing on them (see two pictured —Chapters 13 and 18). Sandy's Black dolls are a fine example of seduction, and she has been seduced by them several times. The poster of a TWA Constellation in Chapter 17 adds to another of our collections, aviation posters. I could go on with painted boxes, small baskets, homespun blankets (and within this collection several in brown (a rarer color than those in the blues), and weathervanes.

Pictured in this chapter are three painted firkins. One sits in each of our three bedrooms. We use them as wastebaskets. We own a smaller one as well. They are a terrific look and complement other pieces. If our home had more bedrooms, I assume we would have a larger collection of firkins of this size. We hope you like them.

Yet I do not think of ourselves as "collecting" painted firkins, but perhaps we do. I think of us as simply owning a bunch of them because they are so functional. I conclude that "three is a collection" is a simple rule of thumb, repeated and believed because most in the American antique community agree with the statement—definition by consensus. Let's see what Nick and Nora find out.

Next, I turn to a known fact in the collecting of American antiques. White is the rarest color for many genres. One sees white on clock faces, in a decorative scheme, but rarely as the primary furniture color. I was informed that Henry Knox of Maine, senior general of the Continental Army and later the US Army, had a set of white Windsor chairs, none surviving to the present. Charles Santore in his books, *The Windsor Style in America, Volumes I and II*, has a photo (Volume II, Plate XI) of a Windsor chair down-scraped to the original white with a wonderful patina. The chair looks great to me, but I am viewing it as a 21st century collector. Nancy Goyne Evans' *American Windsor Chairs* (1996l page 495) notes a later Windsor chair maker (1820s-1830s) with straw and light-colored paint for his rocking chairs was in demand. With white, among other colors, less called for.

In *American Painted Furniture: 1790-1880*, Schaffner and Klein (1997) picture three circa 1820 dressing or fancy work-tables in white and a circa 1810-1830 New England armchair. A very attractive Pennsylvania banket chest, circa 1810, in the same book really pops in white, with scribed geometric patterns in red and dark cobalt blue within divided panels. Consider that almost all the white furniture is Federal, post 1800.

Despite the great numbers of painted Windsor chairs and

other furniture, according to Schaffner and Klein paint was not available in cans ready for use until after the Civil War. It was handmade, not an easy chore. White paint was derived from "lead, chalk and zinc oxide" (page 194). I was surprised to learn that the quintessential white New England church only entered the landscape in the Federal period.

I reached out to well-known dealers with decades of experience. Two themes emerged: (1) white as a color was associated with weddings, and (2) the alleged poor quality of white paint. David Schorsch told me,

> White is most typically associated with so-called bridal furniture of the Federal period to include beds, dressing table and Willard shelf, banjo and at least one lighthouse clock. It is also known on some Windsor chairs made in Salem and other locations circa 1790-1825.

Simon and Aaron Willard produced some gilt frame cases on banjo clocks painted entirely white that Foley states in Willard's Patent Time Pieces are known as "brides' clocks." But no conclusive evidence exists that they were ordered or produced as wedding presents.

The second dealer said:

> The times that white has been used is often related or connected to a wedding. We see white paint decorated mirrors, which has a romantic inclination. Most wedding photographers still today choose to take pictures of the bride in her white (often) wedding dress, gazing into a mirror. We see Classical white frame mirrors, a tradition still followed today. There are 'timepieces' known today as banjo clocks that celebrate weddings with white painted cases. Federal sets of chairs, formal seating fur-

niture are sometimes found painted white and are considered 'wedding furniture'. Titanium white is a type of paint that was an improvement. This color is more stable, doesn't tend to yellow, and was expensive, [though] affordable to prominent families. It is my experience that white paint was accessible in England, not so much in the Colonies. Perhaps another reason for fewer examples of white painted furniture.

A retired paint chemist wrote me the following, also arguing for the poor-quality of white paint hypothesis:

Before I retired, I was a paint chemist. The pigments for good white paint were not readily available in the 18th century. Calcium carbonate was common but did not produce a good white and made a chalky surface that was unpleasant. Inexpensive paints still use a high volume of Calcium Carbonate filler because it is cheap. White lead had the best hiding properties. Titanium Dioxide was expensive and replaced white lead as we learned the hazards of lead. These better white pigments were not available until the 19th century.

Does the poor-quality hypothesis hold? After all, white was used when tinted to produce many other colors.

I spoke with a furniture curator at Colonial Williamsburg who did not know the mystery's answer. She stated some French furniture in their collection had white paint. I also consulted with a specialist in Colonial Williamsburg's furniture conservation laboratory. He refuted the poor quality of white, telling me that other lead-based hues broke down in the same way white did. He commented that some Eastern Shore (Virginia, Maryland) "built in" furniture on occasion (it is still rare) can be found in white. He concluded that lack of white furniture was a matter of style. White simply did not have the "bling" of other colors.

Does the "drab surroundings" hypothesis merit our consideration? More than one collector and dealer believed that the reason white is rare is because people lived in drab, ill-lit settings and wanted color in their lives (other than white). Yet when you see the painted walls, floor coverings, wallpaper, and other uses of color the upper classes lived with long ago, they had color galore. And white is a "clean" color. Yes, it shows the scuff marks and dirt more than robin's egg blue or red, but it is bright, and the item is easily repainted after a. year or two.

Someone else tells me that the color white was expensive. But so much more expensive than salmon, red, yellow, black, red, blue, or green? Because of how it was made did it wear more than other colors? Yet another person wondered if it was stripped from furniture more than other colors.

Would not white furniture or other genres set off something nicely from the brown furniture, yellow chairs, or red blanket chests? It would. Yet white as a primary color is rarer than rare and causes the value of such objects in today's market to soar. I await the report of one of Sam Adams' (of revolutionary war fame) spies and troublemakers to provide me with an answer. Perhaps we may conclude that the primary reason that white is rare is simply because it was never in vogue, never au courant if you will.

A third mystery is the etymology of the term "loper." Yes, I know, "someone who lopes." Lopers are the supports or brackets one pulls out when the lid on a dropfront desk is lowered. My own detective, my elder son Nathaniel, pointed out that Dictionary.com contains the word "loper" stating, "also called draw runner, draw slip. Furniture. Either of the two runners coming forward to support a hinged leaf, as the slant front of a desk." Anyone who collects knows when someone forgot to use them as you see replaced hinges because the lid tore off.

To learn more about the basis of the term, I tried the *Oxford English Dictionary,* and a dusty 1876 edition of Webster's dictionary from the basement of my local library. One wonders the last time it had been touched after Google, and the Internet entered our lives. I posted on a Facebook group, *Americana Hub,* and received some illumination from the latter.

A collector thought that "in the first quarter 19th century it referred to a machine for making rope. I've looked but do not see 19th century or earlier references to the term as a component in cabinetry. It is sometimes called a 'draw bar' though. Puzzling," he said.

Another person commented that the etymology of "interloper" has some clues. Middle Dutch lopen: to run. So ... "runners"? I continued my search. One expert told me that "When I was first in the field in the late 1960s the term was not in use." She wondered if it came into use in "the late 1970s as furniture lingo?" and suggested I contact another respected expert in the field, Robert Trent. Mr. Trent said,

William and Mary period are the earliest such supports, my assumption is that loper meant somebody running, hence the slides or supports were thought to run out. Sometimes seen mis-spelled as 'looper.' The term appears in period bills and account books.

The term then has been in use for quite some time. I wonder if it did not originate in the area that we now call New York City?

The colony of New Netherland was established by the Dutch West India Company in 1624 and grew to encompass all of present-day New York City and parts of Long Island, Connecticut, and New Jersey. A successful Dutch settlement in the colony grew up on the southern tip of Manhattan Island and was christened New Amsterdam. (History.com, August.18, 2021)

I shall hire Adjutant-Detective Henk Grijpstra and Detective-Sergeant Rinus de Gier from the Amsterdam Municipal police to investigate the loper mystery. Someone Dutch may be needed.

Our last mystery of collecting (for now) returns us to collector psychology, this time as a show opens. I have talked with fellow collectors many times about their strategies to maximize the chance they will find a treasure. Some tell me they go directly to the booth or two of dealers who are most likely to have an item in which they are interested. That makes sense to me, a rational decision. Putting these collectors aside, it is then that the mystery unfolds.

Some collectors make a bee line for the aisle furthest from the entryway. Since most people go the other way, they go to the least crowded group of booths (a relative term at a show with a long line). To wit: A friend arrived at a show that had just opened with almost 400 people in line. It took him only 12 minutes to enter the show (a lifetime to some collectors). Another collector chimes in and says one should never go first to the center aisle. He gives no compelling reason but has strong feelings about this. Other collectors go to the right-hand aisle first, the one closest to the show's entrance. They want to ensure they see objects before others who went in different directions.

Three things stand out to me. First, many collectors are strongly wedded to their strategy for finding something at a show and not being beaten to it by someone else. Secondly, every collector knows that once she pauses to look at something in a dealer's booth, 75 people pass her by in those few moments. A third idea strikes me: What is the point? There is no strategy that is best for any one collector. The behavior is superstitious. By that I mean that collectors believe what they do because once or twice the direction they went was rewarded or punished, but the direction each chooses really has nothing to do with his success in being first to the holy grail. Perhaps Sherlock Holmes can send his Baker Street irregulars to several shows, have them employ different strategies, and solve the mystery—does any game plan work best?

There you have it. Four mysteries out of many (I am sure). Does that make them a collection of mysteries? I do not know but I feel better for having shared these with you. You will have to excuse me. I see Bogart, I mean Philip Marlowe at the door. Time to learn which of the mysteries he has solved.

CHAPTER 26

Old Friends

Old friends are precious. Conversations begin as if never left off. They know you well, remember your history and you theirs. They are as comfortable as that flannel shirt or pair of shoes you would never part with. You cannot imagine life without the contact, the laughs, the tears, the ups and downs. You always wish them the very best. Old friends are a deep well of meaning, happiness, continuity, and contentment in our lives. They evoke memories, feelings, and emotions that are important to us. Their friendship is tried and true.

But old friends do not have to be people. Objects as old friends in literature and life are a known phenomenon. In the children's book, *The Velveteen Rabbit*, the rabbit becomes "real" through the love of its owner, and their bond exemplifies the transformation of a cherished toy into a beloved friend. The Velveteen Rabbit is a "transitional object," like a favorite blanket, book or toy that children (even adults) use to soothe themselves during times of stress or transition. Most of us know transitional objects are not limited to childhood. We all form attachments to certain items.

A passionate amateur, Einstein's violin was a source of solace and relaxation for him. He formed a deep attached to his instrument, turning to it for inspiration and comfort, as one might do with an old friend.

Winston Churchill's gold pocket watch was his constant companion throughout his life. It witnessed his triumphs and trials. It is reported that he famously referred to it as his "anchor to reality" during World War II (but I cannot find the source). He named it "the Turnip" but no one knows why. It was his favorite timepiece, a custom yellow gold Breguet commissioned by his uncle John Spencer-Churchill in 1890. Winston was never seen without it.

Why do I bring up old friends? I was thinking of a few of the antiques in our collection that my wife and I have kept despite their cries to be upgraded or that simply do not fit in —inertia, ennui? I think the answer lies more centrally in the notion of old friends, our attachment to objects that ground and center us and have been part of our lives for years or decades.

This old friend is nothing special, except to us. It has been our companion for nigh 45 years. It is a spool cabinet that we use as a small table in the corner of our den, a lamp sits on it, and in its drawers, you will find candles and odds and ends. I am so used to it being there I probably have not looked closely at it for years. A simple cabinet, functional to a fault. It is one of the first pieces we purchased long ago, a bargain at $12 if I remember correctly. It certainly is not high-country and matches nothing else we have collected. Like a tic in my wrist, I do not pay it any attention, but should it disappear, I would notice its absence instantly and regret it. The cabinet is a good deal more than a thing.

Obviously, it is not in original or even near-original condition. When we purchased it, someone had used it as a tool chest and the top two drawers were nailed together. We believe the top should be cherry, but one board is not. The bottom drawer is a replacement. (We were thrilled to find a craftsman to match the existing drawers as it was missing.) It has been refinished. It lacks the inserts in each drawer-front telling someone what may be found inside. From top to bottom: J&P Coates, Best Six Cord, Assorted Colors, White, Black, Spool Cotton.

Why might we keep old friends? Why do we keep this old friend?

Extended Self Theory

According to this notion in consumer psychology, possessions become an extension of the self. Over time, objects like automobiles become infused with personal memories, experiences, and identity. Thus, parting with them can feel like losing a piece of oneself. My wife to this day blames me for our (me?) selling her 1964½ Ford Mustang. I have tried to find her another but cannot. To her it symbolizes independence, youthfulness, and a *joie de vivre*. I think if it appeared in our driveway she would weep. The car and the spool cabinet are part of our life story. They are part of our identities. This spool cabinet reminds us of our early collecting days and the Granary, an antique shop in a town to the north of East Lansing, Michigan.

Our sense of identity and how we approach the world extends beyond ourselves. Objects contribute to these identities, and we all have them, even if they assume different forms. My friend has a daughter whose only talisman is a cast-iron pot her grandmother used to make pot roast. Oddity is no limit. The good-luck silver dollar I have carried for decades honors an uncle who wore one smooth as a pilot of Billy Mitchell bombers in the Pacific in WWII. There is the power suit that gives you confidence. The newel post on the staircase worn smooth from good luck taps each morning.

Nostalgia and Sentimentality

Objects often serve as triggers for nostalgia, evoking memories of significant life events, relationships, and experiences. Research suggests that nostalgia can foster positive emotions and a sense of continuity, contributing to the attachment people feel toward their possessions. I am sentimental about what our kitchen table has seen over the years—oh, if I could only access its observations and two cents worth. It is the example I use in Chapter 10 on grief.

Our two sons ate at that table, first in highchairs and then "big people" chairs. Friends came to visit from Michigan, and six hours later we were still sitting at the table, the homemade chili long devoured, the wine bottles rattling around, empty. Grandmas and grandpas now deceased sat at the table. Good news and not so good news was shared at it over the years. How could we upgrade the table, banish it? We cannot. It is an old friend.

Psychological Comfort

Familiar objects like long-owned cars or American antiques can provide a sense of psychological comfort and security. They represent stability and continuity amidst life's changes and uncertainties. Losing such objects can disrupt this sense of security, leading to feelings of loss and distress.

I know when I walk into our den that I will see our rolltop desk and the spool cabinet. To say the desk does not fit in our collection is an understatement. But we have had it since 1975, and the room would seem empty without it. (Truth in disclosure: It is so practical it would be difficult to divest anyway.)

Circa 1910 oak, C-scroll roll top desk. 60" x 32," 7 drawers, multi-pigeonholes inside roll top, sits on legs, 2 "breadboards."

We can control little in our lives. But collectors can decide that some antiques have become old friends and will remain with them over the years.

The feelings of comfort, security, and continuity such objects offer should not be underestimated. The present tense—see this card table here, a wonderful story accompanies it—offers much more security than, "We used to have a card table; let me tell you about it." Of course, life goes on, of course missing an object is not the end of the world. But it certainly can feel like it sometimes. Just like losing an old friend.

Routine and Habit

Antiques that we own become ingrained in our daily lives. They become part of our routine, that with which we are familiar. Because of this, the ties between us and these possessions may illuminate and increase their significance. I would feel lost without the highboy I have used for decades. I can find the handles to each drawer in the dark. What would I do without the tallcase clocks whose time and strike cords I pull each morning? The ritual also has been ongoing for decades. Old friends indeed.

Another old friend, a small table. There are better ones to be had. But this one has been with us what seems like forever. And despite the finish I must admit I like the color and its lines, the two small drawers, and its scale. It has served us well. Why replace an old friend?

Federal, cherry, 2-drawer drop leaf table, circa 1810-1825. 18¼"w x 15¾"depth top, 8¾" leaves, top extended is 33¼" x 18¼", 29"height. Refinished.

Identity and Self Expression

Objects can also play a role in shaping and expressing a collector's identity. Personal belongings, such as American antiques may reflect aspects of an individual's personality, values, and experiences. These objects become intertwined with the collector's sense of self and may hold significant emotional importance. My wife's Howdy Doody marionette set is a good example. For her, the marionettes are part of her childhood, their emotional importance invaluable. The marionettes do not fit into our collection at all, but they fit perfectly into our identity as collectors. If we ever visited The Antique Roadshow, it is this set we would bring with us.

Circa 1955 Howdy Doody Marionette Set. Peter Puppet Product. Howdy Doody, Clarabelle, and Princess Summerfallwinterspring marionettes. Original box, gallery, instructions, and backdrop. Backdrop colored with crayons. Princess is missing one hand. Otherwise, perfect. Owner since a child.

The literature suggests that our attachment to objects as "old friends" is a complex phenomenon rooted in psychological, social, and cultural factors. Objects can serve as sources of comfort, security, and self-expression, enriching our lives with meaning and nostalgia. Understanding the emotional significance of these attachments can provide valuable insights into human behavior and relationships, and certainly helps explain the outliers in a collection. Such objects may not meet the collector's connoisseurship criteria or even the genres he covets, but they remain old friends.

Our old friends become an opportunity to explain ourselves without talking too personally. Would Sandy be the same person if she did not tote around her Mustang-love, or me if I did not wake every morning, reminding myself to see to the clocks? Things, like relatives and other people, make us unique because they define our limits and horizons (a friend's grandfather's cigars have long defined who he can and cannot stand). Most of "us" is a life-story, isn't it? We need a stage and proscenium to tell it and the things we have, have had, and want to have, are much more poetic than our daily lingo.

By equating objects with old friends, I am anthropomorphizing the latter—steadfastness, feelings we may have of loss if they are no longer present, grief and worry if they are injured. When I began collecting long ago, I never thought I would become so attached to some of the antiques in our home. Do new collectors have a glimmer of what awaits them years later if they continue to collect? I think not. We are stewards of our old friends. In this case less so to preserve material culture or history, but to ward off abandonment if they were to leave us. For there is something comforting about the continuity some of our antiques have provided us over the decades. After all, they are old friends.

CHAPTER 27

Why Some People Do Not Collect

Two roads diverged in a wood, and I—
I took the one less traveled by,
And that has made all the difference.
                    "The Road Not Taken," Robert Frost

In 2018 (in *Maine Antique Digest*) I explored why people collect. Many motivations came to the fore—curiosity, passion, and anticipation among them. I concluded that collecting is a proper and sensible thing to do. Collecting is a quest, it gives people purpose and meaning, it embodies love, joy, and romance, yet also the meaning can be intellectual—connects us to others—and can be competitive. Those who collect Americana when enjoying their collections, can avoid, for the moment, the present. Most important it gives collectors stories to tell, an identity, adventures now and then, and it is fun!

But learning about why collectors collect leaves some questions unanswered. I thought it would be useful to look at those who do not collect to see what insights we might gain. After all, those of us who collect American antiques know many folks who do not collect at all. Focusing on the latter may shed light on why it is we cherish our collecting so, perhaps even be thought-provoking. I let them speak in their own voices, adding only a light editorial hand. By no means do these odes to non-collecting exhaust the Pantheon, but they are a start.

"Russians have 'collectives,' garbage men 'collect' my waste, Catholics speak of the 'collect' of the Mass. So much collection. So common. So extensive. So why don't I collect?

"Let me be honest. I tried, though my friendly critic probably does not give that excuse much credence. I thought I would collect model trains. For a while, I spent time and money buying them. Boxes piled up. Ads came in the mail, on the Internet, from folks who knew of my interest.

"Then I came to a core realization: I am cheap. I enjoy accumulating something, but that is not trains. It is money. There is a fundamental conflict inherent in my condition: To have trains I must lose dollars, and those numbers are incredibly meaningful as far as society and I are concerned. Billionaires take those numbers and buy estates, private jets. Supermodel wives. I just sit and watch and think, 'I could do something with that stuff.' But don't.

"I think people don't collect not because they scorn our history, lack aesthetic sense, fail to appreciate the skill and intensity that went into the creation of that Windsor chair, the sheer luck that allowed the survival of that unique fifty-dollar gold piece in perfect condition over 150 years, the insights preserved in a Hebraic manuscript from the tenth century. When they read of these things in books, look at the pictures, watch the documentaries, they are profoundly impressed. They do not doubt that saving such treasures is worthwhile. Except it is not their job. 'Not on my dollar,' they mutter.

"So, collectors, do your thing. I will stand back and praise you, admire your temerity, respect your expertise. And I'll do my thing: Be cheap."

Another voice makes for a duet. "It is difficult to prove a negative. Why don't you do a lot of things ... ??? Listen to opera?

Have a dog? Bake bread? Collecting never occurred to me. Don't have a hole to fill. I don't feel passionately about things.

"I had a high-powered career that was left brain and sedentary. Collecting seems like more work. I left that behind, interested now in activities that use right brain, not more left brain—physical activities; emotional activities; restful activities. I'm not enamored of stuff for the sake of stuff. I traveled, but it never occurred to me to 'collect,' i.e., get the same thing from each place. I bought reminders of each place, but not the same thing (matchbooks or whatever).

"I had limited time for most of my life. Chose to spend it otherwise. I find that experiences are more important to me than things. Concerts, opera, plays and then dogs, garden, golf, walking, cooking, baking bread, hosting friends on the porch. I seek out social activities. Collecting seems a lonely endeavor. One might say that my philosophical beliefs discourage attachment to material possessions. I find fulfillment in other ways."

The chorale is now a trio. "I hunt and fish and have done so my entire life. The year's passing is marked by opening days. The walls at home are adorned by deer I have shot, bow and gun. I love the outdoors and live for hunting and fishing season. My rods and reels, and guns, are tools to be cared for and used wisely. I see no reason to collect older versions of them. I have no time for such nonsense. My hobbies fulfill me, and I have no room for another. I am passionate about the outdoors. I was upset (not really but maybe) that my son chose to be married during bow season in Wisconsin."

A quartet serenades us. "I grew up in a cluttered home. Those memories are not kind ones, and as an adult I detest clutter, and I identify myself as a minimalist. Material possessions begin to add up and must be cared for. The [fewer] things in my life the happier I am. In my life, less is more. I stay in my lane and probably contribute little to the American economy. I own only essential items and avoid accumulating possessions. I find value in simplicity and decluttering my living spaces. I am the perfect candidate for a tiny house someday. Possessions seem like a burden, an unwelcome reminder of less than sterling days gone by."

We are now a quintet, a small strong group. "I have never thought of collecting. I have school loans, as does my spouse. We have started a family. Childcare is about the same cost as college tuition. Despite being a two-income family, we struggle to make ends meet. Everything seems so expensive. Will we ever be able to afford a home of our own? The car needs a repair. Every penny we have goes to necessities. Perhaps someday but collecting looks like a luxury, one we cannot afford. Financial constraints force me to prioritize other needs and experiences over collecting objects."

Our band has reached six. "Mine is a nomadic lifestyle after the pandemic and Covid. I work remotely and roam the country. Moving frequently, the challenges of transporting and maintaining any semblance of a collection is out of the question. I have a few cherished possessions I put out in whatever living unit I find myself, but a collection, no. Were I ever to settle in somewhere, perhaps? I do not know."

With seven voices we have more timbral depth. "I have a strong environmental conscious and thus avoid collecting to reduce my ecological footprint. I prefer to limit consumption and waste and applaud efforts to recycle plastics, limit harmful emissions, and be a caretaker for mother earth. Many of my friends, who are younger like me, feel the same way. Society produces too many consumable goods of all types. My passions lie in the environmental sphere. I have heard the arguments for buying used goods of all shapes and sizes, but I am not yet convinced."

Another voice has joined the choir. "I have found through-out my life that I move from one set of tastes to another, one set of interests evolve into another. I have been hesitant to commit to a particular collection or genre, knowing I would lose interest or outgrow it. Friends make fun of my home, never quite knowing what new interest has led me to acquire. do not know why the new and fresh attract me, but they do. Then I tire of them. Living with the same objects year after year seems like not living at all."

And yet another. "My life is full of work, friends, com-muting, church, and the minutia of making it through a day or week. I simply do not have the time or energy required to collect something. The task seems overwhelming, a big un-dertaking I am not up for. Stacks of books beckon to me that I never find the time to read. Recipes clipped from here and there, the dishes go unwashed. I find myself part of what is called the 'sandwich generation' with responsibilities to both those younger and elder than I. And when I collapse and find some time for myself, it never seems to last for long before I must rouse myself once again."

One might say these people who do not collect have never been bitten by the bug. They might argue those of us who collect are lucky or could accomplish greater things if we did not. Even if one was raised in a collecting family, it is impossible to argue with those who lack the means or time to carry on the collecting tradition. The world is different than it used to be, more expensive for many than it used to be.

Sandy and I have been bitten by the bug. This Windsor rocking chair, purchased early in our collecting days epitomizes the collecting disease. Its turnings are average. The fact it was always a rocking chair rather than a conversion makes it somewhat rare. It was the first tripleback we owned, and there was something about the form we were smitten with. The black paint looks original and shows appropriate wear. I cannot offer more depth to the statement we were "bitten by the bug." Emotion ruled the day for us back then as young collectors. And we collect still.

Lifestyles are different for many as well—be they $5 cups of coffee, oftentimes costing more to get going in the day, the myriads of lessons and other child requirements, health care, to name just a few. And time constraints cannot be minimized. Those of us who collect consider ourselves lucky, and perhaps we are. Or perhaps there are other ways to live and find meaning we have not yet explored.

CHAPTER 28

Some Thoughts on Being a "Collector"

Who am I? That seems an odd way to begin, I admit, but it is the one question that keeps cropping up most of our lives. Right now, I am a collector, a student, interpreter, observer, and fond owner of antique Americana. But the term "collector" seems slippery, excessively casual, and maybe even deliberately vague.

In conversation, after declaring my *bona fides*, a friend said, "I don't collect anything." I was taken aback: Whenever she visits a national park, she brings home mementos, putting them in a scrapbook. They mean a great deal to her because they preserve and evoke warm memories. I squinted at her and cleared my throat: "That's collecting, isn't it?" I asked hesitantly.

I have another friend whose bookshelf is cluttered with bottles of fine scotch. Unopened. Pristine. He gazes on them affectionately, knows much about how they taste, the region in Scotland where they were distilled, aged, their casks for aging and such. He has not bought a single bottle himself. Friends have given him these as gifts. Behind this display, this collection, lies an irony: While he is a dedicated scotch drinker, he imbibes the cheap stuff. Is he a collector? He would say, "no," that choosing is part of being a collector. I wonder.

How about a woman who inherits a collection of art or American antiques and decides to live with and care for it because of the memories and connections to her family and its past it holds. Is she a collector? When I posed the question, some said she is merely a conservator of the taste of others, some said she is the lucky beneficiary of the goodwill of her forefathers (or foremothers or ...) but some said, of course she is a collector.

This reproduction Chinese ancestral portrait is a departure from our focus on American antiques. It is the object in my grandmother's home that most connected me to her and that I therefore wanted when she died. It is not painted but printed on paper. The cat's haunches repeat as do his snout and whiskers. I do not know the meaning of the background and could find no similar examples when I searched the Internet. Family members in China commissioned ancestral portraits to commemorate deceased relatives, and this may be based on one of them. These paintings were treated with the greatest respect. Traditional ancestral portraits became popular in the Ming (1368-1644) and particularly Qing (1644-1911) dynasties.

My grandmother was not Chinese of course. But I know where and when this came into the family, as you shall hear. The portrait was given to my grandparents as a "freebie" when they purchased some furniture from a store in Chicago during the Great Depression. I never asked my grandmother why she kept it, yet it was displayed prominently in her living room. My wife and I have lived with it for decades. We have never considered purchasing an actual, painted one, or collecting them. The memories this portrait elicits of my grandmother and time in her home when I was a child and then a teen are priceless and powerful.

It struck me that the whole notion of collectors may very well exist on a continuum, from the diehards on one end like me to those much more casual on the other. It is not a question of "what" but "why" (to have your feelings elevated, to learn something new, to capture and preserve a shard of history).

Sometimes people come to shows and auctions dragging a decorator (supposedly someone with refined taste) or the decorator herself may pop up looking for an object or two needed to fulfill an assignment. Dealers are used to this. In these instances, the focus may be more on the appearance of a piece than its provenance, history, or even cost. The decorators' clients may already have several antiques displayed proudly in their home; they need something that complements, not clashes. Antique dealers are realists; they value decorators' business. Are the clients collectors? Alice Winchester, former editor of *The Magazine Antiques* in *Living with Antiques* (1941) calls them "selectors" (page 11), a wonderful term.

I am tempted to adopt a puritanical stance and say, "No, these are mere accumulators, not collectors." We—ahem!— are real collectors, they mere poseurs." That rigidity may be uncalled for, as perfectly respectable commentators have reflected.

For example, "Nathan Liverant and Son Antiques" in an email (April 5, 2022) focused on those looking at pieces for decorating:

And here is something for you to think about. Next time you think about redecorating, consider buying a piece you can enjoy for a lifetime and pass on to your loved ones for more lifetimes. Antiques are aesthetic time machines, and the sentiment they hold binds families and memories. They are sustainable guardians in the home, they tread lightly upon the earth and are solid reminders of history ... The rarity of antiques makes finding the perfect piece feel like a real-life treasure hunt! They offer a polished touch to your home, which cannot be matched by contemporary furniture.

Take that, Ikea!

More than one paragraph has been written about the crying need for more collectors of Americana, especially those who tend younger. One way to hopefully rope them in is to extol and emphasize the "greenness" of collecting antiques. After all, the pieces have existed for a long time, and the planet's ecosystems have not worsened because of their existence. This pitch to those concerned about global warming and the environment has a great deal of validity.

In the same April 5 email "Nathan Liverant and Son Antiques" took just that approach:

Antiques Are The ULTIMATE GREEN! Here is a question for you. If you found an object which would outlast you, your children, your children's children, and their children, need minimal upkeep, would have minimal 'carbon footprint' or drain the earth's finite resources, and was extremely useful to you and uniquely beautiful, would you buy it?

Let us suppose some of these ecologically tickled citizens start purchasing antiques. (I have been told by two very knowledgeable collectors that this is exactly what is happening in Europe.) At least initially they are not inclined to be caretakers for items that centuries have writ large upon. Antiques to them are an often less expensive and more environmentally sound purchase than buying online or traipsing to a furniture store.

"Are these people collectors?" I again ask. Does it matter? They certainly are good for the trade, happy with their purchases, and may convince other, young friends to follow their path. Add to that the fact they are preserving a fragment of history. They may not fully appreciate the piece, but cannot the same be said for some who seriously think of themselves as collectors?

Regardless of their identification, might not these folks develop connoisseurship, a sense of history and as deep a passion, (excitement, joy) for them as we more exalted collectors do?

I specify history, passion, and connoisseurship because I see them as the cornerstone traits of a collector of American antiques. I wonder at the same time, if I am too dismissive of the casual collector. How does one get individuals more interested in and passionate about preventing history from slipping away? Is the stepping over the line from buyer to collector a myth? Is such a metamorphosis an illusion that on cold winter nights warms us with the thought that a future cohort of collectors of American antiques exists?

I reached out to several long-standing dealers and collectors for some insights. The answer to a person was "yes:" Individuals who are given, who casually purchase, who accumulate American antiques regularly become more serious collectors. Kevin Tulimieri, who has been at "Nathan Liverant and Son Antiques" for 26 years as I write this, and still longer now, takes an approach that I am sure many dealers do. Every person who enters his shop or show-booth is looked on as a potential collector, treated with respect, offered detailed descriptions of the pieces and their history. I find his eloquent description wonderfully alive, and his story of the ten-year-old one to treasure.

At our Shop we avoid trying to define people. As they say, you cannot judge a book by its cover. And even when you read a few pages, you can rarely have the complete story. At our Shop we try to engage this natural instinct and innate curiosity. We do this by speaking to people and find out what their interests are. This engagement hopefully develops into a rapport and mutual respect. For us, it is the context and history that brings objects alive and can lead to a deeper level of interest. But really [despite social media] there is no replacement for standing with someone and having a discussion.

We recently have had a young man, about 10 years old, stop by on his way home from school on a few different occasions. The other day he brought a friend too. I enjoyed taking the time to speak with them and share a few quick stories about a 17th century bible box. I had them touch the box and feel the softness of the wood, look closely at the detailed carving and peek inside. This is how we cultivate collectors in our Shop. We share our own passion for these wonderful objects. I approach my engagement with the boy and his friend the same way I approach a discussion with the most advanced collectors at a show. Check this out, look at this detail, have you heard of this person or that family. For me that discussion starts inside, I want to know. I love letting my imagination wander back hundreds, thousands or even millions of years. It is this passion that I hope to share, and if it can spark a similar passion in someone else, that's a huge bonus.

Yet another dealer talked about her strategy in speaking with clients who are using a decorator. When the focus is simply aesthetics and needs, the path narrows quickly. She is insistent in talking about what the piece is, not just how it looks. She wants the buyer to know what this small slice of a very large history means and why it survived.

Do we need then to worry about the future of collecting American antiques? I am told more young parents with children are being seen at shows. Auction houses selling American antiques proliferate. It is as if the marketplace is alive and as Darwin's theories predict, will adapt to ensure its own survival. David Schorsch, a well-known dealer in American antiques, whose mother was a collector and began dealing in American antiques in 1976 said, "No, there was never a concern." In the 1960s people could buy American antiques for the same price as home furnishings, and their quality was superior (we have come full circle). As for the present, he pointed among other things to the Americana auctions in New York City in January 2022 and said, most pieces went to collectors and also spoke of the large number of auction houses that sell American antiques.

Arthur Liverant, also a well-known and in his case third generation dealer in American antiques, told me that the market has always had its ups and downs, most recently the downs include the recession of 2008-09, followed by the Covid pandemic a decade later. He had a strong Philadelphia Show in April 2022, and both dealers and those attending seemed enthusiastic. He pointed out that doomsayers always exists and that the business is "dynamic," mirroring the changing environment. For that reason, marketing must change from years ago and focus on keeping younger people active. He related that his father rarely sold furniture to someone under the age of 35 and that the children of baby boomers now have some discretionary dollars. He was bullish on the future of American antiques. (Of course, others in the American antique world, selling goods at different price points may have a divergent view of what the future bodes.)

And here two paths come together. On the one side, I think being too narrow in our conception of what makes a collector contributes to the sense that the "real deal" types are aging and dying off. If you collect something insufficiently serious—wind-up toys, ray guns, playing cards—you are not as real as we are, you lack critical discrimination. Collecting is a very proper, highly restrictive club.

On the other side, people are ignoring that view. They are buying and cherishing Americana because they like it. They are respectful of craftsmanship, age, significance. Even— yes!—environmental impact. They may not call themselves collectors, but that is exactly what they are, just like us.

The tent of American antiques needs and has room for all sorts of people who have American antiques in their homes. We now must adjust to collectors who show different tastes and impulses than the classic "collectors" did and do. Tolerance must be replaced with enthusiasm. Narrow conceptions of antiques must be stretched to cover a broad variety of genres outside the traditional norms. Good scotch, however, may be more difficult to give a pass.

CHAPTER 29

Divorcing Our Collections

I am standing in line at an antique show, and the conversation fascinates. As is typical, the median age of those in the queue is probably 65 or higher, and the talk turns to divesting our collections. One collector is adamant that she wants top dollar for what she has collected. Another weighs in that he would take less but wants the pieces to be appreciated and enjoyed in their new homes. A third is focused on the collection being displayed and talks of donating many antiques to a local historical society, if only they would not put them in storage. A fourth collector has already begun writing the stories that accompany many of the items in his Americana collection and putting them in drawers and affixed to the underside of tabletops. A fifth wants some pieces to remain in the family, hopeful her grown children and even grandchildren are interested.

They are talking about getting divorced from their collections. Perhaps the divorce will be easy and amicable. Perhaps these collectors will be forced to know themselves—what is it I value and want as we separate? If a couple, each partner may not have values congruent with the other and compromises will be necessary. Mediation may be required—between the collection and the collector, between possibilities in the real world and what the collector hopes for.

I listen, hoping to learn something that will guide my wife and me when the time comes to divorce our own collection. I think of the individual differences of the collectors that surround me, and the psychology of the meaning of being remembered, remunerated, respected, and acknowledged. Anyone who divorces his collection receives value in return. The worth may be measured in dollars, in an emotional impact, in something as simple as "more space" or other outcomes depending on who the collector is. We would expect that emotions and biases would influence this divorce, and they do.

Let us begin with money. Divorces often end up here. An emphasis on money and the meaning of receiving top dollar being paramount must be explored, as it can vary from person to person, and even within the same person depending on the antique being divested. For money often involves a combination of factors—money is never really money. It is anything but.

One dealer in Americana who also works in an auction house told me the following:

> I think when I hear collectors talk about getting "top dollar" what that brings to my mind is obsessing over what every single item in the collection sells for and being willing to expend as much time and energy as they think necessary to do so. And wanting anything back that does not bring their idea of "top dollar" (reserves). I think in practical terms it probably means either highly reserved auction where they babysit every catalog entry, estimate, and reserve, or consignment to a dealer.

Collectors know that top dollar is aspirational and cannot be a certainty. A butterfly flaps its wings somewhere in the world, the stock market sags, and collectors become nervous just as a collector's antiques enter the marketplace. If at auction, despite all his (their) efforts, the antiques may bring a fair price that day, but not top dollar. If pieces are consigned to a dealer(s) patience is called for. Even with superb marketing and the dealer's stellar reputation some pieces may not find a new home for some time, nor at a price the collector hoped for.

Nonetheless, many collectors are motivated to receive a "fair" price. Is doing so as simple as picking an auction house or dealer that (who) is honest and a good fit for the antiques to be auctioned off? Is it as the dealer describes above?

But why an emphasis on money, whether top dollar or not? Here are some potential questions to explore if a collector, or you as a collector, are primarily motivated by money as a collection is divorced.

Investment Value

Some collectors view their art, antiques, or collectibles as investments. They want to maximize their financial return on the initial investment they made when acquiring the pieces. For them, getting top dollar is a measure of financial success.

Financial Security

For some collectors, the funds obtained from selling their collections may contribute to their financial security or serve specific financial goals, such as retirement or funding other projects, interests, or investments. Top dollar represents a means to achieve these financial objectives.

Validation of Taste

The value of American antiques is often tied to their rarity, quality, and historical significance. Getting top dollar for a piece can be seen as validation of the collector's taste and acumen in identifying valuable items. It reflects a sense of accomplishment and expertise in the chosen field of collecting.

Recognition and Status

Inherent in several of the motivations discussed for seeking top dollar for a collector's antiques is that doing so is seen as a source of recognition and status within the collecting community. It may establish the collector as someone with valuable insights and assets, contributing to her reputation among peers. Perhaps the collector wants the auction of the antiques to be a benchmark, talked about by others and the press for years to come.

Preserving a Legacy

Collectors may see their collections as a part of their legacy. Getting top dollar ensures that their carefully curated pieces are appreciated and valued by others even after they decide to part with them. It is a way to preserve and extend the notoriety of their collection. The long-lasting impact of the collection's dispersal is recognized in its fiscal return.

Market Trends

A desire for top dollar may also be influenced by awareness of market trends. Collectors who follow market dynamics may want to capitalize on peak demand or specific trends that can enhance the value of their pieces. This approach is often driven by an understanding of the market and a strategic approach to selling. They want to sell when the market is hot for the genres they own.

Understanding the meaning of money in this context involves recognizing that money serves as a measure of value, providing a tangible and quantifiable representation of the worth of the collector's items. It is a symbol, not only of financial gain but also the broader impact and recognition of the collector's efforts and choices within the collecting community and the wider market.

"All true," I hear you say. "But do not other ways exist to measure worth? I want collectors to have the same emotional attachment to the antiques that we did." Collectors may want to ensure that their cherished items are passed on to individuals or institutions that value and respect their cultural or historical significance, and obtaining top dollar may, thus, not be the prime consideration. Donating antiques to an institution, even with potential tax benefits typically does not equal the monetary return of selling a collection. There are other reasons that collectors who prioritize the excitement and appreciation of the buyer over getting the absolute top dollar for their pieces may feel as they do. Keep in mind that these goals also can be aspirational and may be as difficult to achieve as setting out to maximize financial return. Nonetheless, here are some reasons some collectors might choose to prioritize goals not measured in dollars.

Legacy and Long-Term Impact

Legacy in this context differs from "top dollar" discussions. These collectors want the divorce to contribute to the American antique world. Such collectors may prioritize selling their pieces to individuals or institutions that share their enthusiasm for the items and will actively contribute to their preservation and public appreciation, even if it means accepting a lower price. Thus, they would be hesitant to gift pieces in their collection to an institution if they were to disappear into the archives, to be seen only rarely, if at all.

Building Relationships

The Wall Street Journal had an article (November 2023)

about those selling their homes establishing meaningful relationships with the buyer. In the same vein, building relationships with buyers who share a genuine passion for the items can be rewarding for collectors. Some may prioritize creating connections with like-minded individuals who hold in esteem the collection's value beyond its monetary worth.

Fostering a Positive Experience

Collectors may prioritize creating a positive and memorable experience for the buyer. This could involve sharing stories about the pieces, providing additional context or historical information, and ensuring as best they can that the buyers feel a strong personal connection to the items they are acquiring.

Supporting a Cause

Some collectors may be motivated by philanthropy or supporting a particular cause. They might choose buyers who share their values or who have expressed a commitment to contributing to charitable or cultural endeavors associated with the collection.

Caring Less about Top Dollar

Collectors who are not primarily motivated by financial gain may avoid waiting for the market to peak or the perfect avenues to divesting their pieces to maximize profits, choosing instead to sell at a "fair" price, hopefully to those who genuinely prize the pieces.

Personal Fulfillment

The satisfaction and fulfillment derived from knowing that their collection brings joy and excitement to the new owner can be a significant motivator. For some collectors, the emotional reward of seeing their pieces cherished and celebrated is more important than the highest possible financial return.

Minimizing Stress or Hassle

It can take a great deal of work for a collector or estate executor to disburse a collection. (see the dealer's comments above). Does the spatterware go to a Pennsylvania auction house, the posters to a New York City one, the New England furniture to a New England dealer on consignment, and so forth? Avoiding this lengthy and often complex selling process may entail choosing a smoother and more straightforward transaction, even if it means accepting a lower dollar return.

Fun

Collectors may want to move on from their collections and have fun in doing so. If aged and perhaps infirm they may have enough on their plates than a careful and arduous divorce from their antiques would entail. Pop the champagne, have mirthful conversations with dealers or a chosen auction house, and let the devil take the hindmost. "Life is too short to do otherwise" some collectors may say.

Greater Control

A collector may consign a collection to auction house A that allows her to write item descriptions to ensure their accuracy, and have greater say in the auction catalog even if the terms are less financially beneficial than auction house B.

In brief, collectors can prioritize many variables, e.g., excitement and connection with buyers, over maximizing profits often do so for reasons related to their personal values, goals of long-term impact, and the overall experience associated with passing on their cherished items to new owners. The decision to forego the best price reflects the diverse motivations that drive collectors beyond purely financial considerations.

As might be expected, one finds that divorcing a collection is often not this simple, i.e., the dichotomy between financial and non-financial triumph. A collector or collectors selling their collection can embody many of the above values simultaneously. Some pieces may be earmarked for top dollar, others for appreciation, still others for a legacy within the American antique universe or family. Wanting the statement, "ex collection of ___" to have meaning can depend on price or the taste of the collectors regardless of what their collection brought.

To be sure, a third alternative exists. A collector may be laissez faire about the divorce. Not especially interested in the money side nor the nonmonetary values, a collector may sim-ply want the collection to disappear. "I have run out of space." "I used to have a lot of passion for these antiques, but my ardor has cooled over the years." "Be gone."

"All and good you say," but what sense have you, Dr. Perlman and your wife, made of all these choices and personal needs? After all you are not spring chickens. "What is the end result of your grappling with such a divorce?" "A fair question," I respond, and a good one. It can be better answered by those who have already divorced their collections if we could find their voices to add to our conversation. But I will be a sample of one of those considering the separation.

Let us begin with my wife's collection of novels about girls and women who fly. It has been important to her for some years. It was built tome by tome and doing so took a lot of effort. She has read each and reread some. If her mother was a young woman today, she might have become a pilot. And my wife is a "woman's suffrage" type of person. Only being a pilot will do. So, she was most pleased (and I also) when it appears that we may have found a home for her collection of fiction.

The National Wasp (Women's Airforce Service Pilot) WWII Museum has expressed interest. While nothing is settled, we have our fingers crossed and have not yet explored with them the possibility that the collection be displayed. If so, a small notion with my wife's name would please her greatly. In this case, donating the collection, worth a fair number of dollars supersedes the check we would get if we sold it. In this instance, meaning and sharing is important to us both.

We discovered as we talked that we are not a "top dollar" couple. We would rather the antiques in our collection go to younger collectors of Americana as excited in owning them as we were years ago when we acquired many of them. If not that, then for a fair price, nothing more. We do not view our antiques as an investment but a hobby that has brought great meaning and allowed us to become friends with some wonderful people over the years. It is good enough for us if the collection is fairly marketed and sold by an auction house someday, with perhaps a few pieces consigned to a dealer. If there is a good story or two to tell after the divorce is over, that would suffice.

Nonetheless, questions remain. How does one go about finding excited collectors if that is a goal of letting go of one's antiques? We have not figured that out yet but will make our wishes known to an auction house or dealer. Aside from the books we have no needs for legacy when our collection is disbursed. We do not need the affirmation of a single owner sale complete with a brief biography or page set aside in the auction catalogue, unless that helps brings about a white glove affair (all items in the auction sell).

We would be pleased if a few of our antiques stayed in the family, and our elder son has expressed interest in one or two. We hope they bring him pleasure.

Like the eagle weathervane in the next chapter, this is one antique we will not be divorcing. Our older son has wanted it for some time and figuratively has put a note under the seat with dibs on it. It is a nice piece, with some work done to it that is acceptable given its age. We have lived with it for decades and never thought of upgrading to a "better" armchair of the period. Interestingly, the seat is woven paper. Apparently, paper is easier on the hands of the person making the new seat than rush is. Had we put two or three coats of ochre paint on the seat, it would be largely indistinguishable from an old one. A lesson that all collectors never get around to everything they know they "should" do. We hope our son enjoys the chair.

Of course, collectors aging as they are, do not know what the coming years will bring. But the meaning, or lack of, of their collections is an interesting issue to make sense of, each in their own way. Talking with trusted fellow collectors or dealers may shine light upon the collectors and the divorce. For the collectors' personalities and the significance and essence collectors attach to these pieces of Americana can play a large part in their divorce from them. Photographs might replace visitation rights, seeing items displayed somewhere gratifying. As might the use collectors make of the dollars received for them.

Voltaire observed that "friendship [for our purposes, with the antiques we collect} is the marriage of the soul, and this marriage is liable to divorce." And for some collectors they may feel a part of them has been lost when the process is complete. Yet there is great worth in collectors evaluating who they are and what they value as they divorce their collections. For our purposes, Socrates was correct when he stated that "Knowing yourself is the beginning of all wisdom." But having that wisdom is only half the battle. Actualizing it when a collector divorces his collection may truly be an equal or more difficult task.

CHAPTER 30

Collecting is an Adventure

> Security is mostly a superstition. It does not exist in nature, nor do the children of men as a whole experience it. Avoiding danger is no safer in the long run than outright exposure. Life is either a daring adventure, or nothing.
>
> Helen Keller

Our adventurer sets out, not sure of his return, nor of what he will encounter, traveling to lands beyond. Suffering fatigue and perils, he perseveres. Neither storms, heat, nor angry goddesses dissuade him. He carries no sword, or shield, no means of protection but his wits and experience. "To the glory of the hunt" he sings, as his quest for American antiques recommences.

"Is collecting a 'daring adventure?'" Yes, and a wonderful one. For collecting involves the unknown, seeing what has gone unseen, danger (e.g., poor choices, auction fever, getting snookered), long and arduous treks, uncertain weather, and excitement.

"Fantasy," you say. "Too far-fetched." Years ago, two collectors traveled on their first antiquing trip to New England—pre-Internet, no dealers' wares or auction-house offerings to view online. Their week began with a Northeast Auctions' multi-million-dollar sale. They had never seen a painting sell for close to half a million dollars, the buyer putting it under his arm like a loaf of bread when he went to the desk to pay for it. Then on to the shows. To them, the venues resembled bazars in a foreign land, the entire week unpredictable, romantic, and unfamiliar. Dealers whose ads they had read but whom they had never met. Shows with pieces they had never seen in the flesh, so to speak. Queueing up for hours before a show opened. Decisions to make with no clear outcome. Whose booths to go to first? If I like something on Tuesday, what dollars do I have left later in the week?

One adventurous story from this couple's travels. A blanket chest on Tuesday beckoned. As it did on Wednesday in the same dealer's booth. The show ended; they were too late. But they encountered the dealer at yet another show on Thursday assisting a dealer displaying his wares. The blanket chest? It resided in the dealer's truck awaiting a ride home. Minds finally made up; they purchased it. (The chest is pictured in *Come Collect with Me*). That which they had found and then thought they had lost was theirs ... and still is. And they feel more than ever many years later that collecting is an adventure of the person, perhaps as W. Somerset Maugham said of artists' productions, "the expression of an adventure of his soul."

An adventure is an exciting and daring experience that typically involves exploration, discovery, and overcoming obstacles. A collector explores at auction previews, dealers' shops, and shows. He investigates, inspects, and reconnoiters. He uncovers, brings to light, and finds (to borrow from spaghetti westerns) the good, the bad, and the ugly. He must know the difference between gold and fool's gold.

A collector is constantly faced with challenges, not perhaps as dangerous as the sirens of Greek mythology, monsters such as Cerberus, described as having three heads, a serpent for a tail, and snakes protruding from multiple parts of his body. Cerberus is primarily known for his capture by Hercules, the last of Hercules' twelve labors. I am sure with some reflection I could list a collector's 12 labors. Researching and learning about the genres he collects is one. Knowing the market a second. Surely flying commercially (now there is as a modern-day adventure probably equal to the travels of The Antiquers long ago) a third.

This weathervane is one of two or three pieces our elder son has expressed interest in owning someday. A wonderful adventure underlies his interest, as he is the reason we own the vane to begin with. Nathaniel (the son in question) is a pilot and his first job in aviation had him based in a town so far north in Maine, Houlton to be exact, that we used to joke one needed a passport to get there. At that time, it was a very small town with only one paved road leading in and out. The best restaurant was located at the gas station. Things may still be that way for all we know. Houlton is best known for the northern terminus of the Appalachian Trail and the highest peak in Maine—Mount Katahdin, located in Baxter State Park, just south of the town.

He and I were on an adventure. He wanted to show me the town, and then we could explore a bit of New England while out east. At that time in his life, he owned (actually my wife and I owned the bird, he made payments and took care of it) a 1957 Beech Bonanza. So, he and I set off from Oshkosh about 6 am for the east coast. After two stops for fuel and food we landed in Maine at 2:30 pm. Airplanes truly are time machines. The next afternoon we headed for Connecticut and a dealer's shop or two I had never visited but always wanted to.

At one shop Nathaniel called my attention to the eagle weathervane. He liked it, the way it looked and the reticulated talons on the ball (there is space between the ball and the talons). I did not purchase it then but once we returned home, I thought about it and contacted the dealer. The weathervane was ours. It has a nice surface, a good look to it, and we have enjoyed it for a long time. It sits on top of our highboy in a bedroom, as high as we could place it. We should probably name the eagle but never have. It is truly the result of an adventure with a happy ending.

For the *sine qua non* of collecting is difficulties and not knowing what one will encounter. Trusting love but not letting it lead a collector astray is certainly part and parcel of collecting American antiques. While perhaps lacking in physical dangers, aside from errant elbows at a crowded show, puzzles, riddles, and conflicts arise. Is the piece what it purports to be? Why is it priced so low or high? Is the provenance accurate or made of whole cloth? Why the extra holes in the chest's drawers? Why no signature on the painting? Why is the collector the only one interested in the antique? How can the Hudson Valley painting be almost identical to one the collector owns but unsigned (a true example: The one at auction lacked the details of the DeGrailly hanging on the collector's wall)—the "DeGrailly" was based on a print.

Adventures often take individuals or a group of people on a journey into the mysterious and unrevealed, allowing them to encounter and engage with different cultures, environments, and situations. The unrevealed—Peary or Cook discovering the North Pole (who got there first?). Or the greatest of American adventures, Lewis and Clark mapping and exploring the western frontier of America-to-be.

Welcome to the world of collecting and American antiques. The unknown—an auction or a new genre when the collector's knowledge and research may not be as exquisitely tuned as she would like. Or a new price point that makes the collector faint with anxiety and anticipation. Or a painting by a woman artist lost to history; who was she?

Collectors are acquainted with different cultures, environments, and situations. Not perhaps foreign languages such as Marco Polo encountered on his adventures, or Jane Goodall immersing herself in the world of chimpanzees. The difference between a country auction and Sotheby's or Christies, a culture shock. A country show versus the Winter Antiques Show in New York City. Sipping a warm soda or chilled champaign. The collector finds marked and surprising contrasts between the New Hampshire Dealers' Show and the Delaware Show, small worlds, different worlds, with similarities as well.

Adventures also are characterized by a sense of thrill and

risk. Edward Hillary's conquest (does one truly ever conquer?) Mount Everest, or Livingstone who in 1855 renamed Mosi-oa-Tunya, 'the smoke that thunders', named by the local Batonga, Victoria Falls (for his queen). To some collectors of Americana thrill or risk may equal or surpass the antiques they seek and purchase. Unexpectantly finding a wonderful antique, the outlay of funds on the hunch the diamond is not artificially colored but is truly blue (a true story of a young collector that financed his still ongoing career in jewelry).

Settings play a crucial role in creating a sense of mystery and wonder—the mountain island where King Kong is discovered and captured, the alure of the exotic orient, Dealers booths sometimes are designed to create such wonder. The tent outside the New England home. Box lots auctioned off in their entirety; what will I find within?

Adventures are replete with interesting and diverse characters, oftentimes with unique skills and knowledge. I am told that there were more dealers in years gone by who were "characters," at least they were extolled as such. But in a collector's adventures the number of dealers, auction house folks, and fellow collectors with esoteric bits of this and that are numerous and to be enjoyed. I once talked to a collector who whispered to me about the hundreds of candlesticks he had collected, would I like to see them some day? He would have to trust me more before he allowed a peek.

Adventures carry with them risk, typically to life and limb, or perhaps worse on occasion, one's reputation or place in real or mythical history. The epic poem The Odyssey (Homer), follows the hero Odysseus' ten-year journey after the Trojan War. Odysseus faces numerous challenges, including encounters with monsters, gods, and temptations, all while trying to return to his kingdom of Ithaca. Returning to the Midwest from a trip to New England with my checkbook in one piece and a few pennies to my name does not quite measure up.

Virgil's Aeneid (Roman) is an epic that tells the story of Aeneas, a Trojan hero who escapes the fall of Troy and embarks on a perilous journey to fulfill his destiny of founding Rome. Aeneas faces battles, hardships, and divine interventions during his quest. Many is the time I am sure a collector would welcome (a friendly) divine intervention in his collector's labors but remembers each time when it is was not forthcoming.

The Lord of the Rings (J.R. Tolkien) is a renowned fantasy trilogy follows a group of characters, including Frodo Baggins, as they journey through Middle- earth to destroy the One Ring and defeat the Dark Lord Sauron. This adventure involves battles, alliances, and encounters with fantastical creatures. At times, at shows and auctions a collector can feel right at home in Middle-earth as he battles others to add to his collection. If only the American antique world had a few more fantastical creatures, but perhaps I have overlooked them.

Is my metaphor of collecting as an adventure too far-fetched? I think not. Collectors do not need to follow in Walter Mitty's footsteps with his fantasy and construction. For if collecting American antiques does not quite measure up to Hercules or Marco Polo, the quest for treasure and unraveling mysteries certainly does. For it is treasures that collectors seek—yearning at times for the find of a lifetime. In collecting the quest is never-ending, the collector a hero, now and then, like most mythical adventurers slays the dragon and returns triumphant.

I know it may be difficult for a collector to feel like a slayer of dragons, standing in the rain waiting for an outdoor show to open, or being outbid at an auction for the antique of his dreams. But collectors of Americana do indeed belong in Stevenson's *Treasure Island*, traversing treacherous terrain and difficult obstacles with a thirst for excitement and treasure of their own. To echo Helen Keller, collecting is either an adventure or nothing.

DESCRIPTIONS OF
PICTURED PIECES

Chapter 1 ~ Aesthetic Appreciation: Candlestand

Federal paint-decorated, tilt-top candlestand, circa 1790-1815. New England, probably New Hampshire or Maine, primary wood appears to be birch, 28½" height, top 21¼" x 15½." Overall top painted with central trompe l'oeil paterae, the edge painted with trompe d'oeil stringing, tiling above a ring turned urn-form standard on three highly arched cabriole legs, the surface grain painted to imitate mahogany. Original paint, wooden catch also original.

Chapter 2 ~ Heart and Soul: Dial of Tallcase Clock

Circa 1830 wooden works tall case country clock, pine, 87½" height to top of middle finial, 19" wide bonnet, 17½" wide base, 13¼" wide at waist, 6 7/8" depth waist, 8¾" depth base, 9 5/8" depth bonnet. Signed S. Hoadley, Plymouth (CT). Dial is in excellent condition, hand painted with a paddle wheel boat in the crest, an American eagle is incorporated in the Hoadley signature. Thirty-hour wood movement is in running condition. There is restoration to the wood gears. The movement appears to be the original movement to the case. The pewter hands are original. Weights and pendulum are both replaced. The pine case has the original black paint with simulated gold inlay and trim with restoration to the black paint (black overpaint over original surface) and the trim (repainted). The base is original and has not been cut down. A coat of varnish was applied to the case to preserve the existing paint. The original fretwork was repaired. The finials are cast brass. Pull on door is a replacement.

Chapter 3 ~ Satisficers and Maximizers: Blanket Chest

Mid-19th century American, 6-board blanket chest. Probably New England but perhaps Ohio. Simple high-country style, 40½" wide, 17½" depth. Wrap-around moldings on raised base. Nice side cutout on base. In original dark blue paint, butternut with poplar secondary wood. Repair on hinge and minor restoration to the molding around the lid.

Chapter 4 ~ Personality: Child's Chair

Circa 1680 1720 child's-size William and Mary ladder back mushroom armchair with unusual turned crest rail and flame stitch needlepoint upholstered seat. Eastern Connecticut or Rhode Island. In good condition retaining a fine historic painted surface with black paint over an early or original red, with the black paint added in the mid-19th century.

Chapter 5 ~ Resilience: Black to Move Painting

Circa 1850 folk art media, "Black to Move" of an old Black woman playing checkers with a young Black girl. Signed C. Tipp, Original ornate gold frame, 12½" x 15" framed; picture is 5⅝" x 7½." Superb condition. The dealer from whom we purchased the painting stated that the picture presents folk art created for the sole purpose of merging two media—to take a print and embellish it to create a three-dimensional illusion, sometimes referred to as decoupage in the art world. To bring forth this charming portrait of Black sitters is a unique use of this folk-art technique. Yet when we look closely at the work it looks like it is painted with no visible signs of decoupage.

Chapter 6 ~ Wondering: Robert Walter Weir(?), *Boston Harbor from Across the Bay*

A 1827 plaque centered at bottom of painting on the frame reads: Oil on canvas. Original frame, 24" x 30½" framed, painting is 18¼" x 25⅜." Superb condition. Lightly cleaned. Painting is attributed to Robert Walter Weir. Stylized trees in his manner. I cannot find a listing of this painting among Weir's works—it may be undocumented. I would like a second opinion. Restored. Original stretcher accompanies the painting.

Robert Walter Weir (June 18, 1803 – May 1, 1889) was an American artist and educator. He is considered a painter of the Hudson River School. Weir was elected to the National Academy of Design in 1829 and was an instructor at the United States Military Academy. His best-known works are The *Embarkation of the Pilgrims* (in the Rotunda of the United States Capitol at Washington, D.C.) and *Landing of Hendrik Hudson.*

Robert Weir was born to Robert and Mary Katherine (Brinkley) Weir on June 18, 1803 in New York City, (It is commonly reported that he was born in New Rochelle, New York, however the family did not move to New Rochelle until 1811). Weir never graduated from college, and in 1821, at the age of 18, he left a job as a mercantile clerk to pursue painting. He studied art in New York City from 1822 to 1824, teaching himself drawing and painting, before departing in 1824 to study in Italy. He remained in Florence studying Michelangelo, Raphael, and other Italian masters of the Renaissance. Weir returned to New York in 1827 to care for a sick friend. He remained in New York until 1834 and became an integral part of its artistic community. He was then appointed as Teacher of Drawing, later Professor of Drawing, at the United States Military Academy at West Point, New York.

Replacing the late Thomas Grimbrede, Weir was the fifth artist to hold the position of art instructor at the academy. During his 42 years (1834–1876) in this post, he instructed many of the future commanders of the American Civil War, most notably, James Abbott McNeill Whistler and

Seth Eastman. He also developed a special relationship with Ulysses S. Grant. He died in New York City on May 1, 1889.

Chapter 7 ~ Awe: Thomas Chambers, *A View of the Hudson from West Point*

Circa 1840 Hudson Valley oil on canvas painting. *A View of the Hudson from West Point* by Thomas Chambers (1808-1866). Active New York/New England. Unsigned, 18" x 24," 23½" x 29½" with frame. Fine condition, lined, with very minor scattered in-painting. Period but perhaps not original frame. This was a popular and desirable view that Thomas Chambers liked to paint depicting a view of the Hudson River with sailboats looking down river from West Point. This example has a warm, colorful palette with a few American flags flying on the masts of the sailboats, complimented by Chambers' distinctive style for painting trees and mountains. It graces the book's cover.

Chapter 8 ~ Failure and Losing Out: Tiger Maple Chest of Drawers

Circa 1780-1800 American Chippendale tiger maple five drawer chest on straight bracket base with excellent cutouts on the side, 36" wide, 18" depth, 44" height (case). Top is 39¾" wide, 19¾" depth. Molded top, two boards, with wonderful overhang. Top two drawers open as one. Brasses are replaced Ball & Ball best thin coat brasses. Top replaced. Excellent condition. Refinished at some point in time.

Highchair

Circa 1760 Connecticut slat-back child's highchair, with two-way splayed legs in wonderful untouched original painted surface. No restoration or repair. The top front stretcher shows centuries of use, 33" height.

Chapter 9 ~ Gratitude: Redware Banks

Circa early to mid-1800s, 4" to 7¼" height. Matte to high glaze finish.

Chapter 10 ~ Grief: Kitchen Table

Circa 1860 maple drop leaf kitchen table, 42" length, 23" wide, leaves are 12½" length, table is 42" x 48" with leaves extended. One drawer round turned legs, original wooden knob.

Chapter 11 ~ Joy and Contentment: Victor DeGrailly, *Highlands Gorge, West Point, New York*

Circa 1850 Oil on canvas painting *Highlands Gorge, West Point, New York* by Victor DeGrailly (1804-1889). Lived/active: New York and France. Unsigned, 14$1/8$" x 20," 21" x 27." Great condition, minor touch-ups in sky, appears to be original carved giltwood frame. Provenance: private collection. New England Auctions, CT. Victor DeGrailly was among one of the more prolific Hudson River School artists. Most of his works were based on engravings from Henry Bartlett's book, *American Scenery*, published in 1840. He had a real fascination and interest with the Hudson Valley. This painting clearly represents his work showing figures in the foreground and an expansive view of the Hudson with boats.

Chapter 12 ~ Love and Desire: Dining Room Table

Circa 1730-1760 Queen Anne Walnut Table. Originally sold from a family in Portsmouth, NH. All original including an old dry finish. Cupid bow ends. 52" x 57," 19" wide with leaves down. Purchased some time ago at Northeast Auctions.

Chapter 13 ~ Euphemisms: Money Wanted Redware Loaf Dish

Circa 1830 Norwalk, Connecticut, 143½" x 10¼" redware loaf dish, *Money Wanted.* Coggled rim, fine condition.

Chapter 14 ~ Good Luck: Watercolor, *View from West Point-Hudson River*

July 18, 1843 *View from West Point-Hudson River.* Watercolor on paper, 19¾" x 26¼," sight size 15½" x 21 ¾." Frame not original to the piece, labeled for a Canadian frame shop that opened in 1874. Signed lower right by the artist Sarah J. Stoddard. Excellent condition, colors present as bright and bold. Minor spotting not detrimental to the painting.

Chapter 15 ~ Marketing: Small Basket

Nineth-century oblong basket, 7½" length, 5½" wide, 4½" at the handles. Wood splint with carved handles and wrapped rim. Very dry original apple green paint. Condition is very good with minor losses.

Chapter 16 ~ Seduction and the Casting of Spells: Smutt the Cat Painting

A1977 primitive painting of yellow cat. Signed on back, Norma Bury, 17¼" x 13¼." Oil on canvas, maple frame.

Chapter 17 ~ Serendipity: TWA Constellation (Connie) poster

A 1952 poster, Frank Soltesz artist, 25" x 40." Linen backed. A condition. Exceptional bird's-eye view of TWA Constellation flying over lower Manhattan and the Statue of Liberty at dusk. *TWA—Tran World Airlines. Flying is the Way to Travel—And TWA is the way to Fly.* One of the most beautiful of all aviation posters. Rare.

Chapter 18 ~ A Week in the Life of a Collector: Prudance and Temperance Redware Loaf Dish

Circa 1825-1865 slip-decorated redware rectangular loaf dish featuring the inscription: "Prudance & Temperance." Norwalk, Connecticut, 13¾" x 8¾." Red clay body with white-yellow slip decoration under a clear glaze. Provenance: The distinctive yellow color of the slip and glaze and the style of script writing are frequently found together in redware coming from the Norwalk area. The design can be compared to a slip decorated redware plate inscribed "Norwalk, Feby the 13, 1854," illustrated in *Ceramics in America 2004, "It's quarter to Twelve ... and Way Too Late* by Richard Prowse, Figure 16. While the "Norwalk" plate has been previously attributed to the Asa E. Smith property, active 1825 to 1888, the author suggests that current research supports Smith as a stoneware potter and the traditional slip decorated Norwalk redware was crafted at a different pottery.

Chapter 19 ~ Do What You Want to Do: French pitcher

Circa 1850 French Jaspe ware pitcher, 3½" height, 3" diameter.

Chapter 20 ~ Finds: English Silver Teapot

1902 English silver teapot. Charles S. Green & Co, Birmingham, England. Excellent condition.

Chapter 21 ~ Pitfalls in Making Good Decision: Pair of Candlesticks

Circa 1740-1760 pair of Queen Anne push-up candlesticks, Brass, English, 8 ¾" height. No repairs.

Chapter 22 ~ Quitting: Small Round Pantry Box
Circa 1900 round pantry box, 3 ½" diameter, lipstick red.

Chapter 23 ~ A World Gone By: Rush Holder
Circa 1780 rush light.

Chapter 24 ~ Displaying Antiques to their Best Advantage: Horse and Sulky Weathervane
Circa 1890 Horse and Sulky Weathervane attributed to Cushing and White, Waltham, MA, 18½" height, 37" wide, 5" depth. Full body molded copper, cast, zinc, iron (spokes). Excellent condition, traces of sizing and historic gilt surface now worn with oxidation. Original reins, whip, and spokes. In a wonderful compact size with great form and motion. This horse and sulky weathervane has survived in a remarkable state of preservation. Note the attention to the fine details such as the cast head of the jockey and canted high wheels. Picked at Brimfield, 2024, sold to a dealer and then sold to us.

Chapter 25 ~ Four Mysteries: Three Firkins
Late-19th-century firkin, 9" cover size, 10¼" height, 9½" bottom diameter. Pointed bands, copper nails, original dark green with old red over green on top and body. Excellent condition.

Circa 1880 New England, dark green firkin, all original, 9" depth x 9" height.

Late-19th-century firkin, 9" cover size, 9 ¾" height, 9 ½" bottom depth. Pointed bands, copper nails, original gray-blue paint. Cover stamped LYB. Excellent condition.

Chapter 26 ~ Old Friends: Spool Cabinet
Circa 1900 six-drawer solid cherry spool cabinet, 26" wide, 19" depth, 22" height. Cherry top, white porcelain

knobs (replacements), turned columns on either side of the bank of six drawers, one drawer is a replacement, refinished.

Chapter 27 ~ Why Some People Do Not Collect: Tripleback Windsor Rocking Chair

Circa 1800 tripleback Windsor rocker. Black paint, original throughout, always a rocker. Construction typical of Tracy (Windsor, CT). But the turnings are not up to Tracy's standards.

Chapter 28 ~ Some Thoughts on Being a Collector: Chinese Ancestral Portrait

Circa 1935, 25½" x 41½." Sight 1½" x 32½." A reproduction Chinese ancestral portrait. The rank badge in the center of his robe depicting a phoenix indicates that he is a Civil official. Bamboo or bamboo looking frame. Grass cloth matte or grass cloth appearing matte. Given to my maternal grandparents when they purchased furniture in Chicago. Printed on paper.

Chapter 29 ~ Divorcing our Collections Slatback Armchair

Early-18th-century ladderback armchair. Four-slat, best finials, medial arm stretcher, early base stretchers, old but not original paint, new rush seat, ended out, repaired break to one stile, 48 ½" chair height, 17" seat height.

Chapter 30 ~ Collecting is an Adventure: Eagle Weathervane

Circa 1890 Horse and Sulky Weathervane attributed to Cushing and White, Waltham, MA. 18 ½" height, 37" width, 5" depth. Full-body molded copper, cast, zinc jockey head, iron (spokes). Excellent condition, traces of sizing and historic gilt surface now worn with oxidation. Original reins, whip, and spokes. In a wonderful compact size with great form and motion. This horse and sulky weathervane has survived in a remarkable state of preservation. Note the attention to the fine details such as the cast head of the jockey and canted high wheels.

INDEX

ABOUT THE AUTHOR

Baron Perlman is a long-time collector of American antiques and other genres. When young he began with stamps, baseball cards and comic books. Oh, if he had only kept the latter. Collecting is what he does.

Born in Chicago Perlman attended Lawrence University (Appleton, WI) and Michigan State University where he earned his master's and doctorate in clinical psychology. His MSU sojourn was interrupted by service in the U.S. Army, including a tour in Vietnam.

As a clinical psychologist he worked in the Department of Psychology at the University of Wisconsin, Oshkosh and consulted. He spent a lot of time listening and "making sense of," both of which have served him well as a collector and author. He is now joyfully retired.

His interests in collecting and writing have led to numerous columns in the national publication, *Maine Antique Digest*. In 2019 he published *Come Collect with Me: Musings on Collecting and American Antiques*. And in 2021 his second book saw the light of day, *The Collector's World: More Musings on Collecting and American Antiques*.

Married 53 years, his wife Sandy joins him in collecting. They have lived in flyover country, Oshkosh, Wisconsin, for what seems like an impossibly long time and have two sons and two cats. Neither son nor the cats are as consumed with collecting and writing as their dad is.

If you enjoyed this book, reviews on your favorite book website are greatly appreciated.

www.ingramcontent.com/pod-product-compliance
Lightning Source LLC
Chambersburg PA
CBHW051137120626
46547CB00012B/842